THE ROYAL HORTICULTURAL SOCIETY
PRACTICAL GUIDES

HARDY
PERENNIALS

THE ROYAL HORTICULTURAL SOCIETY
PRACTICAL GUIDES

HARDY
PERENNIALS

RAY EDWARDS

DORLING KINDERSLEY
LONDON • NEW YORK • SYDNEY • MOSCOW
www.dk.com

LONDON, NEW YORK, MUNICH,
MELBOURNE, DELHI

PROJECT EDITOR Cangy Venables
ART EDITOR Margherita Gianni

SERIES EDITOR Pamela Brown
SERIES ART EDITOR Stephen Josland

MANAGING EDITOR Louise Abbott
MANAGING ART EDITOR Lee Griffiths

DTP DESIGNER Matthew Greenfield

PRODUCTION MANAGER Patricia Harrington

First published in Great Britain in 1999
Reprinted 2003
by Dorling Kindersley Limited,
80 Strand, London WC2R 0RL

A Penguin Company

03 04 05 10 9 8 7 6 5 4 3

A CIP catalogue for this book is available from the British Library.
ISBN 0 7513 47205

Reproduced by Colourscan, Singapore
Printed and bound by Star Standard Industries, Singapore

See our complete catalogue at
www.dk.com

CONTENTS

HARDY PERENNIALS IN THE GARDEN

WHAT IS A PERENNIAL?

TAKEN LITERALLY, THE TERM "perennial", used in botany, embraces all plants that produce vegetative growth for at least three years – that is, anything from a daisy up to a tree. However, when it is applied to garden plants, it usually refers to herbaceous plants: those with growth that does not become woody, except perhaps around the base or "crown" of the plant as it matures.

HARDINESS TO COLD

Hardy perennials are those that are able to survive freezing temperatures without protection and, as a group, are some of the most valuable plants to the gardener in cool temperate climates. Some are best replaced after three or four years in favour of young, fresh specimens; others remain vigorous for up to 30 years. Most cope with severe weather by dying back in autumn, the crown and roots remaining dormant safely below ground until the temperature rises once again in spring. Some perennials are described as evergreen, but in fact are not strictly so; their leaves and stems are simply tough enough to remain intact in winter. They are replaced by fresh growth in spring, when most gardeners prefer to trim off the previous year's growth which, although it may have survived, has generally become tatty through the physical effects of weathering: for example, freezing and thawing of the tissues, the weight of snowfall and wind.

▶ CENTRE STAGE
In small planting areas, groups of perennials can create tapestries of flowers and foliage.

◀ LASTING SHOW
Year after year, perennials can contribute summer colour and texture to every garden, whatever the site and soil conditions.

Most perennials are not difficult to grow and look after, and there is an enormous variety to choose from. The majority will adapt to less than perfect conditions; some will positively thrive in the most "problematic" of sites, such as a shady corner or in an area with permanently moist soil. They come in an enormous range of sizes, colours, textures and shapes, making it possible to create all kinds of designs and effects that will suit even the smallest space. Their diversity makes them ideal for every style of garden, and there are many that are just as at home in containers as in the open ground.

CHOOSING HARDY PERENNIALS

The choice of hardy perennials is so great that you could fill the largest of gardens with nothing else, yet still enjoy almost 12 months of interest (see pp.12–19). Most gardeners are drawn to perennials for their huge range of flower forms and colours,

STRIKING SCHEMES
Theme borders need careful planning and siting, but the results can be dramatic. This bed, mainly composed of asters, penstemons and chrysanthemums, glows with colour in late summer.

but remember that interest comes from foliage, too; leaves and grasses can look extremely effective, especially when frost covers dying stems and dry seedheads.

GROUPING PLANTS TOGETHER

In most gardens, perennials are simply one element among other types of plants (see overleaf). But planting schemes consisting

> The sheer diversity of perennials makes them ideal for any garden style

solely of hardy perennials, carefully chosen to grow well together, can be beautiful and long-lasting. Later in this book you will find a number of planting plans that suggest groupings for various sites and in various styles; all are designed using plants that will, hopefully, be readily available, but a good garden centre will be able to suggest alternatives – or, make your own choices from the *Recommended Perennials* section (pp.65–77). Notes, and even the roughest plan of what you think you can

◄ ISLAND LIFE
*Use perennials of different
heights to create a herbaceous
landscape in island beds.*

▼ BRIGHT IDEA
*Pots filled with variegated
grasses can be used to
brighten up a dull corner.*

achieve in the space and on the site and soil
available, will help enormously when
buying plants. In small gardens this is
particularly important.

PLANTING STYLES AND IDEAS

Few sights are finer than a traditional,
well-stocked herbaceous border (*see p.27*),
especially when set against a formal clipped
hedge or attractive wall or fence. A more
informal look can be achieved by allowing
cottage garden or naturalistic plantings (*see
p.33*) to break out of border constraints
and spill over paths and lawns. Low-
growing, creeping, herbaceous perennials
give interest to dull expanses of paving and
soften the edges of brick, gravel or
concrete paths. An island bed with an
informal curving outline is another option.

Lots of perennials have fragrant flowers,
and some have aromatic foliage: position
these where you can enjoy their scent.
Many make good cutting plants, yielding
flowers for the home. Others grow well in
containers, easy to place where you can
appreciate them at close quarters: on the
patio, for instance, or close to a door.

BREAK FROM THE BORDER
*Bleak expanses of gravel, concrete or paving
may be softened by allowing low-growing
perennials to spill out from borders.*

MIXED PLANTINGS

OVER THE PAST CENTURY, shrinking garden size has had an effect on the way perennials are used. Nowadays, few people possess a garden large enough to incorporate large, traditional borders devoted entirely to herbaceous perennials. Consequently, these plants are more likely to be interspersed among shrubs, bulbs and annuals to create mixed plantings, which can be planned in a formal style but often tend more to what romantics term a "cottage garden".

CREATING STRUCTURAL INTEREST

Integrated planting increases the height range in borders, extends seasonal interest and is usually much less labour-intensive than a scheme devoted solely to herbaceous plants. Existing beds and borders may already have a complement of shrubs, which will retain their shape, and sometimes their leaves, all year. Shallow-rooting perennials that are not too greedy for food, like geraniums, make wonderful "skirts" for the bare lower stems of roses.

SHELTER AND HEIGHT
Walls and fences provide useful sheltered sites for warmth-loving perennials, and provide support for a backdrop of climbing plants.

In established gardens, borders may be overshadowed by woody plants. Partial shade suits many herbaceous perennials; dense shade, however, will seriously restrict your choice: consider removing or thinning some old trees and shrubs. There's usually no harm in politely asking neighbours if they would consider thinning theirs.

If starting a garden from scratch, place trees and shrubs first, with taller ones at the back and lower ones at the front. These can also be used as hosts for climbing plants; other freestanding climber supports, such as poles or tripods, can help enormously to provide height in exposed beds, where delphiniums and other tall perennials might suffer from wind damage.

◄ FILLING OUT THE BORDER
*Hardy annuals, like these blue nigellas, make
excellent fillers for any gaps that appear
between perennials (here iris and alliums), and
frequently self-seed themselves.*

▼ THEMED MIXED PLANTING
*Group plants of different types that enjoy
similar conditions: this hot and sunny scheme
contains gladioli and shrubby cistus with
felted verbascums and feathery crambe.*

ANNUALS AND BULBS

Lightweight, annual climbers like canary
creeper (*Tropaeolum peregrinum*) can be
planted to twine among robust perennials.
Hardy annuals mature quickly and can
usually be sown directly where they are to
flower, either in the early autumn or spring.

Sow hardy annuals as gap-fillers while perennials are still small

---

They make excellent gap-fillers while
perennials mature. They will sometimes
self-seed, reappearing the following year:
you can weed them out or keep them,
depending on where they are growing.

Spring bulbs can be used to create
brilliant combinations, not only with early-
flowering perennials but with the fresh
colours and textures of their newly
emerging foliage. The bulbs' leaves will die
down to yield the stage to summer plants.
Containers full of late spring- and summer-
flowering bulbs, such as lilies, and of half-
hardy bedding plants, also make very
effective stop-gaps, useful when unexpected
casualties occur or for covering bare areas
of ground where foliage from spring-
flowering bulbs has been cleared away.

PERENNIALS FOR SPRING

T RADITIONALLY, PERENNIALS ARE USED to give their finest display in summer, yet there are plenty that are valuable for spring interest. One of the best reasons for planning planting groups carefully is to ensure that there are plants that are good to look at at all times of year spread evenly throughout the scheme, and complementing other types of plants such as bulbs and shrubs.

A RENEWAL OF GROWTH

Hellebores are the first perennials to flower in the year. The glistening white flowers of Christmas rose *(Helleborus niger)* appear in late winter, followed by the Lenten rose *(Helleborus orientalis)* in a medley of white, pink and purple shades, with many of the flowers delicately spotted and splashed on the inside.

As winter gives way to spring, the pace of growth accelerates. Trim away old, scruffy foliage of perennials that has persisted through winter to let all the beauty of the young growth shine through. Most early-flowering herbaceous perennials are low-growing, so position them at the front of beds and borders. Plant them in

groups to make substantial clumps, with interplantings of early spring bulbs; later, the fading bulb leaves will be hidden as the plants grow. In early spring, blue and white-flowered lungworts (*Pulmonaria*) are early flowering favourites, along with the taller growing Siberian forget-me-nots (*Brunnera*). Many of the former have attractive silver-splashed and spotted foliage, while several variegated forms of the latter are ideal for brightening up shadier spots in the border. Cool, fresh colour combinations can be achieved by mixing them with small spring bulbs such as white snowdrops and blue scillas and grape hyacinths. For warmth, yellow and cream-coloured globeflowers (*Trollius*)

▶ FRESH FLOWER CLUMPS
A clump of brunnera holds court at the front of the spring border, surrounded by crowds of admiring scillas.

▼ FIRST TO BLOOM
Creamy hellebores and blue pulmonarias signal the return of spring to plantings of hardy perennials.

NEW GROWTH
The fresh, new foliage of perennials emerging in spring – here hostas, stachys, tanacetum and lupins – makes a lovely textural foil for flowering bulbs such as these tulips, their white purity echoed in the leaf margins of the variegated hosta.

quickly follow, along with the pink and crimson hues of bergenia flowers, many still resplendent in coppery winter foliage.

By late spring borders are swinging into colour, much of it provided by old-fashioned favourites including leopard's bane (*Doronicum*), columbines (*Aquilegia*) and foam flower (*Tiarella*). If you are hoping that some perennials will have self-seeded, be careful on early weeding forays: while some plants, including columbines, are quite distinctive from an early age,

Watch out for self-seeded perennials on spring weeding forays

others, such as honesty, are rather coarse-leaved and can easily be mistaken for interlopers. Give plants a chance to reveal their identity: you will soon come to recognize the villains.

The foliage of established summer-flowering perennials will be burgeoning, providing a lovely setting for later spring bulbs such as tulips and narcissi planted in the border, or becoming a focal point in its own right: verbascums, for example,

produce steadily rising towers of whorled foliage that draw the eye for weeks before the first flowers open.

Some early spring-flowerers will by now be assuming the role of low, foliage plants, ideal for ground cover. Other plants, such as dicentras, will continue to bloom from late spring well into summer; some flower in succession for even longer (*see below*). In small gardens and restricted spaces, these are among the most valuable perennials, providing a display that begins in spring and continues through the season as neighbouring plants change and develop.

PERSISTENT FLOWERERS

Perennials that will start to bloom in spring and should then continue to produce flowers off and on throughout the season include:

Aquilegias	**Geum**
Centranthus	**Malva**
Dianthus	**Mimulus**
Diascia	**Polemonium**
Epilobium	**Sidalcea**
Geraniums	**Symphytum**
Filipendula	

Deadheading and removing stems of spent flowers (*see p.56*) can also encourage many plants to prolong their flowering display.

PERENNIALS FOR SUMMER

As SPRING GIVES WAY TO SUMMER, rising temperatures will encourage a surge of growth and, above all, a profusion of flowers. The number of summer-flowering perennials available is vast, but where space is at a premium it makes sense to choose varieties that, as individuals, provide both flowering and foliage interest and, collectively, a continuous succession of colour.

HEAT AND LIGHT

Intense colour is a feature of many summer-flowering perennials, whether it be the short-lived, blowsy beauty of rich pink and red Oriental poppies and peonies, or the longer-lasting, shimmering blue haze of salvias and nepetas. As the season progresses, warm colours can easily dominate, as orange- and yellow-flowered daylilies (*Hemerocallis*) compete with red-hot pokers (*Kniphofia*) and crocosmias. Whether you find a general fiery effect stimulating or stifling is entirely a matter of

personal taste. You can play it up, adding plants with bronze or purple foliage, or temper it by including pastel shades, such as pink-flowered *Geranium* × *oxonianum* 'Wargrave Pink', or a contrasting selection of blue or white flowers – the blue-tinged white flowers of *Campanula persicifolia* 'Chettle Charm' are ideal – and the occasional dash of steely or silvery foliage.

To get the best from summer perennials, site them where their flowers and foliage can be seen to their best advantage. Plants with deep colours, especially brilliant reds

▲ A CLOSER LOOK
Summer provides a range of lovely flower forms to compare and contrast: here, bold peonies and clusters of delicate aquilegias.

▶ TURNING UP THE HEAT
The bronze-leaved dahlia 'Bishop of Llandaff' provides a stunning backdrop to yellow flowers and foliage.

▲ FRESH AS A DAISY
Rudbeckias give a spectacular show of flowers throughout late summer and autumn. If possible, plant in bold drifts.

◄ LIGHT RELIEF
Break up rich drifts of blue (here from lavender and campanulas) with fresh green ferns and steely eryngiums.

and oranges, often look best when given a prominent spot in the sun, whereas strong sunlight can bleach out pale colours. White and pastel shades light up shadier positions, and whites and blues become almost luminous as dusk deepens: these are the colours to plant on and around patios, or wherever you like to sit on summer evenings. These are also spots where some

---

Scented plants in pale, luminous colours enhance evenings on the patio

---

fragrant plants, such as dictamnus and oenothera, are a must, whether you are entertaining in your summer garden or simply relaxing after a hot day's work.

Borders in exposed sites, on very free-draining sandy soils, are most likely to dry out in summer, so here it pays to give priority to heat- and drought-tolerant perennials. Planting trees and shrubs to provide some shade will help less resilient plants ward off the effects of strong sun, but remember to adjust your choice of plants accordingly: too much shade will reduce the number and quality of the flowers of many sun-loving plants.

PLANTS FOR DRY PLACES

You can improve the moisture-retentiveness of light, dry soil (*see pp.51, 54*), but good plant choice is also essential. Plants that will still put on a show in hot, drought conditions include many with tuberous or thick roots, such as echinops, poppies, irises and sisyrinchiums, together with those with succulent leaves and stems (such as sedums) or grey, downy or hairy leaves: anthemis, artemisia, nepeta, osteospermum, phlomis, stachys. Grasses, with a small leaf surface area that minimizes water loss, also stand up well.

PERENNIALS FOR AUTUMN

FAR FROM BEING A SEASON OF DECLINE, autumn can provide a curtain call for all the colours of summer. Indeed, many of the late-summer border perennials break through seasonal boundaries to give a succession of valuable flower and foliage interest until the first touch of frost. Foliage, grasses and seedheads also play their part in broadening the autumn colourscape, with the leaves of many perennials changing colour as temperatures drop.

THE DAISY FAMILY

Perennials with daisy-shaped flowers, such as asters, echinaceas, heleniums and rudbeckias, many of North American origin, are great standbys for late summer and autumn. Perennial asters in particular make a superb show in shades of blue, lilac, cerise, pink and white. All types of *Aster × frikartii*, such as lavender-blue 'Mönch', may well be in flower from mid-summer until at least mid-autumn; in mild districts, even later. Other asters, such as semi-double, rich red *Aster novi-belgii* 'Royal Ruby', provide a lower-growing but equally prolific show for weeks in late summer and early autumn.

PLANTING FOR COLOUR

Sunflowers (*Helianthus*), bronze or yellow heleniums, yellow rudbeckias and orange-centred pink echinaceas keep the warmth

▲ AUTUMN FAVOURITES
Asters, especially mauve ones, are also known as Michaelmas daisies, after the traditional mid-autumn saint's day of the same name.

▼ LATE SHOW
Fantastic flower displays are possible in autumn: ribbons of pink asters are punctuated here by black-centred golden rudbeckias and the arching yellow plumes of goldenrod.

▲ LANDING PADS
*The flat flowerheads
of sedums are a late
treat for bees and
butterflies.*

◄ THINK PINK
*Clump-forming
Japanese anemones
will spread to form
drifts of fresh, pink
and white flowers.*

of summer in mind as autumn closes in. Goldenrod *(Solidago)* is another cheerful plant that spans the seasons, and the taller varieties make a fine yellow flower foil for blue asters. Most solidagos, however, tend to be rampant colonizers, so choose carefully unless you are trying to fill a large area of wild garden. Golden-yellow

---

The leaves of many perennials change colour as temperatures drop

---

S. 'Laurin' is one of the best for smaller borders, as it does not grow to more than 60–75cm tall, with an initial spread of around 45cm.

In shady areas the beautiful pink or white chalices of Japanese anemones look superb, and the autumn display would be incomplete without at least one or two hardy chrysanthemums. Nor should some of the less well-known perennials be overlooked. Bugbane, *Cimicifuga simplex*, for instance, adds a graceful touch with its arching wands of small white flowers.

When autumn gives way to a mild winter, growth can continue and it can be hard to decide when perennials have "finished" and should be cut down. There are no strict rules: as long as you are still enjoying a plant's appearance, you can delay tidying it up, even until spring.

AS WINTER APPROACHES

Autumn is a time for tidying herbaceous perennials, cutting back growth ready for the dormant season, but the stems and, particularly, seedheads of some plants are worth keeping over winter for interest *(see overleaf)*. Consider leaving in place until spring:

Achillea	Hakonechloa
Astilbes	*Lunaria rediviva*
Carex	Miscanthus
Cortaderia	Phlomis
Echinops	Sedums
Eryngiums	Stipa

Prolonging the Season

As winter approaches, you could be forgiven for thinking that borders can only present a rather bleak picture. Yet cold weather often turns an otherwise boring outlook into a superb panorama, with frost riming every available surface, and the low sun silhouetting the shapes of "freeze-dried" stems and seedheads. The paucity of hardy herbaceous perennials in flower during the colder months can be offset by the use of evergreens.

Winter Interest

Give those perennials that are in flower, such as hellebores and the beautiful winter-flowering *Iris unguicularis,* foils of solid foliage colour: dark evergreen shrubs, for example, or bergenias, particularly those whose green summer leaves turn red with cold. Evergreen ground-cover perennials such as bergenias and epimediums not only relieve the bareness of borders in winter, but also give protection from harsh frosts to the crowns and roots of plants below ground. Don't forget "ever-grey"

SHOWN OFF AT THEIR BEST
Give those perennials in flower in winter, such as these Helleborus foetidus, *a strong back-ground – here the young red stems of cornus. Against a variegated shrub, their subtle flower colour would be dissipated and lost.*

perennials, too: felt-like, silver-leaved *Stachys byzantina* will sparkle when frost gathers on its plush leaf surfaces.

Perennials with warm foliage colour are very welcome. The colours of some grasses, such as yellow-striped *Carex oshimensis*

Evergreen ground cover will relieve the bareness of borders in winter

---

'Evergold' and red-tinged *Hakonechloa macra* 'Aureola', persist, while others dry and fade to buff shades. Their stark forms, together with seedheads of plants such as eryngiums, phlomis and sedums, are among the most beautiful sights in the winter garden when touched by frost.

▲ SHELTERED SCENE
The delicate-looking but surprisingly tough plumes and spikelets of grasses may persist through autumn and winter, dried to warm browns and beiges: if they are given some shelter, as here by shrubs, their stems will suffer less from battering by winter winds.

◄ FROSTED FORMS
Phlomis, asters, fennel and, to the rear, a clump of miscanthus are among the plants left uncleared in this border, creating a perfectly preserved winter landscape glistening with frost.

PERENNIALS FOR COLOUR

COLOUR WHEEL

DO NOT BE AFRAID to experiment with colour – the possibilities are endless. Choose combinations that appeal to you, rather than something you think you ought to like. Use the principles of the colour wheel (*left*) to explore the way in which colours are related, and why different types of colour combination can create such different effects.

THE COLOUR WHEEL

The wheel in its simplest form comprises three primary colours: red, blue and yellow, which, when blended together, produce the secondary colours between them: purple, green and orange. Infinite gradations of shade and hue occur where the segments meet. Colours furthest apart on the wheel contrast the most. The principle opposites occur between primary and secondary colours; purple and yellow, red and green, and blue and orange. Such combinations can produce bold and dazzling effects, and are especially impressive when viewed from a distance. Some plants create their own vivid contrasts: the bright green leaf-fans and brilliant scarlet flowers of the crocosmia 'Lucifer', for example – but plant associations can be equally intense. Grouping blue-purple *Salvia × sylvestris*

COLOUR CONTRASTS
Grouping together dissimilar, or directly contrasting, flower colours can be visually exciting. The violet campanula, for example, makes the yellow hemerocallis appear dazzlingly bright, while the purple-blue of the Ajuga reptans, seen with the tangerine-coloured geum, appears intense and vibrant. White, on the other hand, is perceived as reflected light in its purest form.

MECONOPSIS BETONICIFOLIA

TROLLIUS × CULTORUM 'ALABASTER'

LEUCANTHEMUM × SUPERBUM

PAPAVER ORIENTALE 'MRS PERRY'

ASTER AMELLUS 'NOCTURNE'

'May Night' with yellow *Oenothera*, for example, will excite the eye and accentuate the individual richness of their colours.

Using neighbouring colours – pink *Papaver orientale* 'Mrs Perry' with purple nepeta, perhaps – creates soft, harmonious combinations. From a distance the effect

In a red-themed border, will you include orange or crimson – or both?

may be a little hazy, but close-up it will be subtle and elegant. Warm groupings of reds, orange and gold (*see overleaf*) come to meet the eye, while cool purples and blues (*see pp.24–25*) create an illusion of distance. Planned colour-themed plantings can be

spectacular, expecially if you manage to maintain a continuity of colour throughout the season. Remember, when planning on paper, that varying heights are particularly important when few colours are used. When listing plants to look out for and buy, note their heights too, so that any substitutions you choose or have to make will maintain the form as well as the colour theme of your scheme.

FOLIAGE COLOUR

Unusual leaf colour plays a part in the most intriguing combinations: gold, lime, blue-grey, silver, copper and purple. The way we perceive colour is also affected by texture and light: yellow-splashed foliage, or fine silver or golden grasses, for example, give the illusion of dappled sunlight, and lift colours around them.

CROCOSMIA 'LUCIFER'

GEUM RIVALE 'TANGERINE'

CAMPANULA CARPATICA

EUPHORBIA SCHILLINGII

AJUGA REPTANS 'ATROPURPUREA'

HEMEROCALLIS 'CONDILLA'

USING HOT COLOURS

EVEN IN THE COOLEST OF SUMMERS, an illusion of warmth can be produced from plantings incorporating a liberal sprinkling of bright yellow, orange and red flowers. There are only a few fiery shades available for spring display, but colours intensify quite noticeably during summer months, with warm gold and russet tones becoming increasingly prominent with the onset of autumn.

A GLOWING YEAR

Doronicums and primulas are among the first perennials to make a sunny splash in spring, but it is the summer that ushers in the most dazzling hues. One of the first is *Geum* 'Borisii', which produces orange-scarlet flowers in early summer, sometimes with a later flush of coppery-hued blooms. Other easy choices include orange and red oriental poppies, red peonies, crocosmias in fiery red, orange and gold, and daylilies *(Hemerocallis)* in every hue of yellow, orange and rust-red. Shortening days

BRINGING THE COLOURS FORWARD
The free-flowering crocosmia 'Emily McKenzie' makes a lasting display, especially effective when set against yellow or purple.

encourage sedums, whose flat, rich rose-pink flowerheads are borne in profusion from late summer to autumn, together with heleniums, in yellow or the bronze-red of 'Moerheim Beauty'. Yellow rudbeckias may continue to flower until cut down by frost.

Bronze or purple foliage intensifies hot flower colours

Warm colour shades usually complement one another, so you can plant a selection of perennials to create distinct "hot spots". Orange and bright red shades also look particularly effective when set against a foil

▲ POWERFUL COMBINATION
The warmth of the orange daylilies exaggerates the cool purple of the agapanthus, making the daylilies appear closer than they really are.

► CONTRASTING FLOWER SHAPES
A variety of flower shapes is provided by this vivid collection of rudbeckias, monardas, dahlias and tall-growing kniphofias.

of coppery-purple leaves; the bold foliage of *Rheum palmatum*, for example, though it is extremely large. In a small space try clump-forming *Heuchera micrantha* 'Palace Purple', with metallic, dark purple leaves.

Some plants even provide their own foliage foil, such as moisture-loving *Lobelia* 'Queen Victoria', with blazing red spikes over beetroot-hued foliage, and *Lychnis* × *arkwrightii*, sporting vermilion flowers set against purple-bronze leaves.

RECOMMENDED

SPRING-FLOWERING
Doronicum 'Miss Mason'
Oenothera fruticosa 'Fyrverkeri' ♀
Primula rosea

SUMMER-FLOWERING
Achillea filipendulina 'Gold Plate' ♀
Crocosmia × *crocosmiiflora* 'Emily McKenzie'
Hemerocallis fulva 'Flore Pleno'
Kniphofia triangularis ♀

Lychnis chalcedonica ♀
Monarda 'Cambridge Scarlet' ♀
Paeonia officinalis 'Rubra Plena' ♀
Papaver orientale 'Allegro'

AUTUMN-FLOWERING
Helenium 'Butterpat'
Lobelia cardinalis ♀
Rudbeckia 'Herbstsonne'
Sedum 'Ruby Glow'

USING COOL COLOURS

THE FRESHNESS OF SPRING can be enhanced and mid-summer heat relieved in part by planting perennials in cool shades. Blue and white schemes are the obvious choices but can be stark; a sprinkling of restrained hues such as pale yellow, greens and soft pinks enhance the effect. Cool shades can also be combined with contrasting colours to produce deliberate clashes.

KEEPING IT COOL

Cool schemes are easy to carry through the spring and most of the summer, starting with white and pink-flushed hellebores, perhaps supplemented by wood anemones, white and blue varieties of *Primula denticulata*, soft pink or white bergenias, and the Siberian forget-me-not *(Brunnera)*. These are followed by pink, blue or white campanulas, blue or white monkshoods *(Aconitum)*, hardy geraniums in every shade of blue, purple, pink and white, and catmint, *Nepeta × faassenii*, which produces aromatic, grey-

> Cool colour schemes can be enhanced with silver or white foliage plants

green leaves topped by soft lavender-blue flowers. Colours tend to heat up in late summer, but it is possible for beds and borders to keep their cool with plenty of foliage and elegant, white-flowered Japanese anemones.

HEIGHT OF ELEGANCE
Flower spires in cool shades give a fresh, airy look. The odd warmer hue, here from the verbascum 'Helen Johnson', *will not intrude among* (from left) *delphiniums, campanulas and dicentras.*

BORDER HIGHLIGHTS
Lime green flatters hot colours, but also adds freshness to cool schemes: here, euphorbia and alchemilla are set against a dark background.

ALSO RECOMMENDED

SPRING-FLOWERING
Aconitum 'Bressingham Spire' ♥
Anemone nemerosa (wood anemone)
Bergenia 'Silberlicht' ♥; *Helleborus foetidus*
Primula denticulata var. *alba*
Pulmonaria saccharata 'Argentea' ♥

SUMMER-FLOWERING
Alchemilla mollis ♥; *Campanula* 'Burghaltii' ♥
Geranium pratense 'Mrs Kendall Clark' ♥
Leucanthemum × *superbum* 'Esther Read'

AUTUMN-FLOWERING
Anemone × *hybrida* 'Honorine Jobert' ♥
Cimicifuga simplex 'Elstead' ♥
Eryngium oliverianum ♥
Ergyngium variifolium

HIGHLIGHTING THE EFFECT

An almost snowy scene can be achieved by restricting your choice of plants to those producing white flowers; alternatively, plant only blue-flowered subjects for an even chillier display. The cooling effect can be further emphasized by adding silver- or grey-leaved foliage plants, several of which conveniently produce flowers in complementary shades. The prickly-leaved sea hollies (*Eryngium*) with white or silver foliage and blue and silver flowerheads are good examples, as is felt-leaved *Stachys byzantina* 'Silver Carpet'. A non-flowering but evergreen plant, it can be used in white or blue planting schemes and makes an excellent mat of silver-grey ground cover.

COOL COMPANIONS
This subtle blend of cool flower colours is further enhanced by the aromatic bronze-purple fennel foliage.

PLANTING PLANS FOR PERENNIALS

CHOOSING PLANS AND STYLES

THE BEST RESULTS (and least work) are achieved by choosing schemes that blend well with their surroundings and contain plants that are naturally suited to the conditions imposed by the site. A plant that needs moisture, for example, will never be happy in poor, fast-draining ground, and will need scrupulous watering in a terracotta pot. The following pages contain planting ideas that will work equally well in urban or rural settings, and have been designed for a range of environments from sun to shade, and poolside to trough.

TRADITIONAL BORDER STYLE

A well-planned herbaceous border can provide a breathtaking panorama of colour from spring until the first frosts of autumn. Until quite recently, such borders were planned on a lavish scale, integrating bold drifts of flowers with bands of attractive foliage. Today, it is perfectly possible to adapt the style for smaller gardens, and using carefully chosen perennials that suit your site and soil will cut down the time needed for maintenance. You will need to include plants of varying heights; to minimize the need for staking, choose compact, self-supporting varieties of tall plants where available. Plants with interesting foliage will contribute to the display even when not in flower.

▶ TENDING YOUR BORDER
For a traditional look, plants are kept neat and are not allowed to flop. Twiggy sticks (right) make unobtrusive supports, and will not spoil the look of the border. Removing dead flowerheads (far right) *regularly helps to encourage further flowering on many plants and keeps the border looking tidy.*

PROVIDING SUPPORT (*P.55*)

PROLONGING FLOWERING (*P.56*)

◀ POSITIONING PLANTS *Well-packed plants limit the space in which weeds can appear.*

A TRADITIONAL HERBACEOUS BORDER

This long, narrow border in sun contains fairly easy-going plants for an average soil, its texture improved by good preparation (*see p.50*). Yellow doronicums and pink bergenias make an early display; they have finished flowering in this illustration (*continued overleaf*). Campanulas, lychnis and anthemis follow on closely behind, then the flamboyant crocosmias which, with asters and helianthus, keep the show going in late summer.

PLANTING PLAN

1 3 × *Anthemis punctata* subsp. *cupaniana* ♥, 35cm apart
2 3 × *Aster novi-belgii* 'Little Pink Beauty', 45cm apart
3 4 × *Lychnis chalcedonica* ♥, 35cm apart
4 2 × *Campanula glomerata* 'Purple Pixie', 30cm apart
5 1 × *Helianthus* 'Loddon Gold' ♥
6 3 × *Bergenia* 'Baby Doll', 30cm apart
7 3 × *Crocosmia* 'Lucifer' ♥, 35cm apart
8 2 × *Doronicum* 'Miss Mason' ♥, 45cm apart
9 2 × *Aster × frikartii* 'Mönch' ♥, 40cm apart

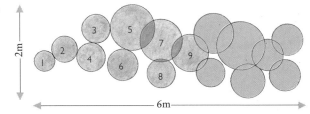

2m

6m

Aster novi-belgii 'Little Pink Beauty' will produce better flowers if you thin some shoots in spring (see p.56).

Anthemis punctata subsp. *cupaniana* produces its daisy flowers throughout summer if given a sunny site. The silvery leaves are also decorative.

Lychnis chalcedonica is an erect plant that needs no staking. In summer it produces heads of star-shaped, scarlet flowers.

Bergenia 'Baby Doll' has pink flowers in early and mid-spring that gradually darken with age.

Helianthus 'Loddon Gold' is a perennial sunflower that adds height to the border.

Crocosmia 'Lucifer', with its strong arching stems, is one of the easiest crocosmias to grow.

CAMPANULA GLOMERATA 'Purple Pixie' starts to flower in early summer. Deadheading prolongs its season.

ASTER × FRIKARTII 'Mönch' is an excellent cultivar of this long-flowering and disease-resistant aster.

Doronicum 'Miss Mason' bears bright yellow daisy flowers in mid- and late spring, held high above the foliage.

TRADITIONAL BORDER *continued*

Verbascum chaixii 'Gainsborough' bears stately spikes of light yellow flowers over woolly foliage.

Achillea filipendulina 'Gold Plate' forms evergreen clumps of grey-green leaves. A few flowerheads, produced all summer, could be sacrificed for dried arrangements.

Helenium 'Coppelia' has copper-orange flowers that give the border a warm glow from mid-summer to early autumn.

DIANTHUS 'MRS SINKINS'
A well-known, deliciously scented, old-fashioned pink. When plants become scruffy, renew them by layering (see p.61).

PLANTING PLAN

10 3 × *Helenium* 'Coppelia',
  45cm apart
11 3 × *Dianthus* 'Mrs Sinkins',
  30cm apart
12 2 × *Verbascum chaixii*
  'Gainsborough' ♀,
  45cm apart
13 2 × *Sedum* 'Ruby Glow' ♀,
  35cm apart
14 2 × *Echinops bannaticus*,
  90cm apart
15 3 × *Achillea filipendulina*
  'Gold Plate' ♀, 60cm apart
16 2 × *Salvia* × *superba* ♀,
  45cm apart

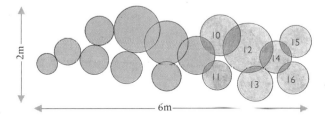

MORE CHOICES

Other relatively easy-going
perennials well suited to the
formally-kept style are:

CLUMP-FORMING
Alstroemeria ligtu hybrids ♀
Aquilegia McKana Group
Echinacea purpurea 'Robert
  Bloom'
Hemerocallis 'Golden
  Chimes' ♀
Heuchera 'Pewter Moon'
Gypsophila paniculata
  'Bristol Fairy' ♀
Monarda 'Croftway Pink' ♀
Nepeta 'Six Hills Giant'
Paeonia lactiflora 'Bowl of
  Beauty' ♀
Papaver orientale
  'Perry's White'
Phlox paniculata 'Prince of
  Orange' ♀
Physostegia virginiana
Scabiosa caucasica 'Clive
  Greaves' ♀
Sidalcea 'Elsie Heugh'
Stokesia laevis 'Blue Star'
Thalictrum delavayi
  'Hewitt's Double' ♀

SPIKES AND SPIRES
Delphinium 'Blue Nile' ♀
Iris 'Early Light' ♀
Kniphofia 'Royal Standard'
Liatris spicata 'Kobold'
Lupinus 'The Chatelaine'
Schizostylis coccinea
  'Major' ♀
Veronica 'Shirley Blue' ♀

FOLIAGE INTEREST
Artemisia 'Powis Castle' ♀
Eryngium bourgatii
Euphorbia griffithii
  'Dixter' ♀
Phlomis russeliana ♀
Stachys byzantina 'Silver
  Carpet'

*Additional details can be
found in* Recommended
Perennials, *pp.64–77.*

*ECHINOPS BANNATICUS
The hairy, grey-green leaves
surround woolly stems topped
by bluish-grey flowers that
will attract butterflies and
bees to the border from mid-
to late summer.*

Salvia x superba has spikes of
purple flowers that contrast in
shape and colour with the
neighbouring achillea.

Sedum 'Ruby Glow' softens the border's edge
with its fleshy, purple-green leaves and soft
red flowers at the end of summer.

NATURALISTIC PLANTING

Traditionally "tidy" borders appeal to orderly-minded gardeners, but hardy perennials also lend themselves to a wilder, more informal style. Almost any perennial can be used in this way, but careful grouping is needed to achieve even the most artless-seeming effect. The plan overleaf has been designed to create a manageable small border; repeating some of the plants elsewhere in the garden creates the impression that they have spread naturally.

CREATING AN INFORMAL EFFECT

Don't be cautious; use bold perennials, such as rudbeckias and goldenrod in asymmetrical drifts, with low-growing, self-seeding plants such as alchemillas as dense ground cover to suppress weeds around taller plants. These will need to be robust to resist being swamped by the spreading plants. Wild species are often bigger than named varieties, with a greater proportion of foliage to flowers: this can also look more natural than highly-bred, floriferous plants in unexpected flower colours.

PERENNIALS IN GRASS

The meadow look is much coveted, but establishing perennials in grass is not easy. For a much more manageable planting, simply include some ornamental grasses (*see box overleaf*) among perennials. Plant them in groups to create natural-looking ribbons and drifts of grass surrounding the flowering plants. These grasses and the flowering plants will compete on equal terms for the nutrients and moisture in the soil, and identifying and removing perennial weeds will be much easier.

▶ NATURAL COLONIZERS
Opportunist self-seeders such as aquilegias soon fill gaps between purchased plants, heightening the informal effect, in which plants are allowed to spread, and reducing the space available for weeds.

◀ PROVIDING GREENERY *Macleayas (here with campanulas) are valuable for foliage interest.*

PLAN FOR AN INFORMAL BORDER

This plan, shown in mid-summer, includes easy-to-grow perennials, tolerant of a variety of soils and a degree of summer neglect. Apart from two irresistible cultivars of geranium and plume poppy (*Macleaya*), it comprises more naturalistic-looking species plants. Foliage interest is supplied by architectural plants such as acanthus and macleayas, while the inclusion of grasses echoes the latest trends in garden design.

PLANTING PLAN

1 1 × *Acanthus mollis*
2 3 × *Geranium pratense* 'Plenum Caeruleum', 60cm apart
3 3 × *Rudbeckia laciniata*, 60cm apart
4 3 × *Athyrium filix-femina* ♀, 50cm apart
5 2 × *Macleaya microcarpa* 'Kelway's Coral Plume' ♀, 90cm apart
6 1 × *Carex pendula*
7 5 × *Leucanthemum vulgare*, 30cm apart
8 2 × *Campanula latiloba*, 45cm apart
9 3 × *Aquilegia vulgaris*, 30cm apart
10 2 × *Briza media*, 50cm apart

Acanthus mollis has handsome leaves and flowers that develop into polished seeds of the same rich russet as conkers.

Rudbeckia laciniata has deeply cut leaves and yellow flowers with central cones of greenish-yellow.

GERANIUM PRATENSE 'Plenum Caeruleum' is a double-flowered version of the geranium that grows wild in meadows. Its foliage colours well in autumn.

Athyrium filix-femina, the lady fern, forms a delicate pool of green fronds.

USING ORNAMENTAL GRASSES

Most ornamental grasses are unfussy and can be treated just like other perennials, cutting them back in spring to remove tatty growth, being careful not to damage emerging leaf tips. There are silvery and gold-leaved grasses; even some with banded foliage that give the illusion of dappled sunlight. Their waving movement gives a lovely, naturalistic effect. More and more small, clump-forming grasses are becoming widely available. Miscanthus (*right*) and cortaderia can form very large clumps: a row of these as a hedge-like backdrop to an informal border is useful for breaking up wind in an exposed site. *For more details, see p.71.*

M. SINENSIS 'ZEBRINUS'

Macleaya microcarpa 'Kelway's Coral Plume' adds hazy height to the planting with its clouds of tiny flowers.

Leucanthemum vulgare bears simple daisy flowers in late spring and early summer.

Carex pendula, a tufted, evergreen sedge, gives year-round interest, especially if the drooping seedheads are left on the plant.

Campanula latiloba makes evergreen basal rosettes of foliage from which shoot spires of blue bells in summer.

Briza media, the quaking grass, adds texture both with its foliage and its oat-like seedheads.

...gia vulgaris, or ...bine, will scatter ...eds with abandon.

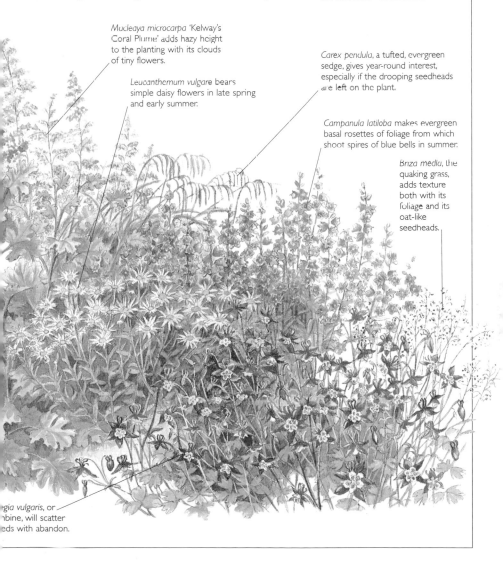

PLANTING IN SHADE

Some shade is always an asset in the garden, and there are many hardy perennials that will not only tolerate but positively thrive in a site sheltered from all-day sun. The degree of shade, however, will affect what you can grow; as the depth and period of shade increase so the choice of plants decreases. The planting plan overleaf shows a range of flowering and foliage plants that will all thrive in shade, and lists some alternatives.

DEALING WITH SHADE IN THE GARDEN

The density of shade can vary greatly. Under deciduous trees, you can make the most of the light early in the year to grow colourful bulbs among other spring-flowering plants. In dappled shade, where trees and shrubs are not densely planted, or in areas that the sun reaches for only part of the day, cyclamen, violas and primulas can provide spring interest, and summer perennials such as astilbes and aruncus will flower well. Generally, only foliage plants can cope with the day-long, year-round shade cast by evergreens or tall buildings. Here, ferns and hostas come into their own, and combine well with bronze-leaved bergenias and spotted pulmonarias.

PRACTICAL TIPS

• Trees and shrubs overshadowing perennials will also compete with them for food and water. Water young perennials regularly until they are established, and mulch areas in the rain shadow in spring while the ground is wet. Plants may also benefit from a balanced fertilizer. This must not be applied, however, when soil is dry or it may damage plants.

• A wall or tree that casts shade is also likely to create a rain shadow. Check that plants have sufficient water during dry spells.

• Plants in the shadow of a dull, dark wall will immediately look brighter and livelier if the wall is painted white. The wall will reflect light into the area, cheering it up and also benefiting the plants.

SPRING PLANTS UNDER A DECIDUOUS TREE
Naturalized bulbs flower beneath a deciduous tree before it has come into leaf; their leaves will die back into the wild grass for summer.

SPRING PLANTS IN LIGHT SHADE
Early-flowering primulas and violas will carpet the ground around shrubs and will appreciate their shade later in the summer.

◀ GREEN PARTNERS *Blue-green hostas and ferns are great standbys for shade.*

PLAN FOR A SHADY CORNER

This planting capitalizes on the fact that shaded soil often holds moisture well, but drier soil can be mulched (*see p.54*). The chalice flowers of hellebores are frequently in full display by mid-January, quickly followed by the clustered blooms of bergenias. Pink, blue and white are the dominant summer flower colours, with more interest introduced by a yellow foxglove, the textured hostas and purple-green fern fronds of athyrium.

Polygonatum falcatum 'Variegatum', a stripy-leaved Solomon's seal, adds an elegant arching shape to the planting.

Polystichum setiferum is a tall, evergreen fern, useful for providing colour and architectural interest during winter.

HELLEBORUS ORIENTALIS
Cup-shaped flowers, sometimes spotted, open from mid-winter to early spring. Cut away old, tattered foliage which detracts from their beauty.

Omphalodes verna has bright blue flowers that can be vulnerable to a late frost.

BERGENIA 'SILBERLICHT'
A vigorous cultivar with leathery, evergreen leaves and white flowers in spring that age gracefully to pink.

Brunnera macrophylla has forget-me-not-like flowers in spring. It self-seeds prolifically.

Athyrium niponicum var. *pictum* has fronds suffused with purple, green and silver-grey.

Hosta sieboldiana has huge leaves and later produces pale lilac flowers.

PLANTING PLAN

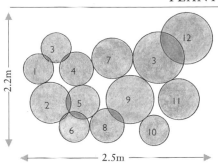

2.2m

2.5m

1 2 × *Omphalodes verna*, 45cm apart
2 1 × *Bergenia* 'Silberlicht' ♥
3 3 × *Digitalis grandiflora* ♥, 30cm apart
4 3 × *Polygonatum falcatum* 'Variegatum', 30cm apart
5 1 × *Helleborus orientalis*
6 2 × *Brunnera macrophylla* ♥, 45cm apart
7 3 × *Polystichum setiferum* ♥, 30cm apart
8 2 × *Athyrium niponicum* var. *pictum* ♥, 45cm apart
9 1 × *Hosta sieboldiana*
10 4 × *Tiarella wherryi* ♥, 25cm apart
11 1 × *Dicentra spectabilis* ♥
12 2 × *Campanula latifolia*, 60cm apart

Campanula latifolia produces deep violet or white bell flowers in summer.

Dicentra spectabilis produces its locket flowers in late spring and early summer.

Tiarella wherryi has clouds of small, pinkish flowers in late spring and early summer.

DIGITALIS GRANDIFLORA
This unusual foxglove has pale yellow flowers in early to mid-summer above clumps of evergreen leaves.

MORE CHOICES

FOR DRY SHADE
Carex pendula
Iris foetidissima
Lunaria rediviva
Paeonia emodi

FOR MOIST SHADE
Matteuccia struthiopteris
Meconopsis
Osmunda regalis ♥

AS GROUND COVER
Anemone × hybrida
Pulmonaria
Polypodium vulgare (fern)

PLANTING IN DAMP GROUND

Plants that need free-draining soil will not only fail to thrive but often rot in damp ground, but there are plenty of attractive perennials that relish a constant supply of moisture at their roots. Many tolerate seasonal flooding, but unlike true aquatic species, most dislike having wet feet all the time. If you love these plants, yet do not have a suitable spot for them, a plastic-lined bog garden (*below*) is not only easy to make but very water-efficient.

CONSTRUCTING A BOG GARDEN

The edges of informal pools (*see overleaf*) are prime sites for bog plants, but it is also easy and inexpensive to create your own bog garden. Excavate a bowl-shaped hole at least 45cm deep. Rake the area, remove any sharp stones and line with thick plastic sheeting. Pierce the base of the liner in plenty of places with a garden fork to prevent excess waterlogging, and cover with a 5cm layer of garden (lime-tree) grit. Fill up with a soil mix (*see below*), then water thoroughly before planting.

PRACTICAL TIPS
- If the surface of the soil seems dry, it's time to top up the water.
- A thick mulch of bark or chippings over the soil when wet helps slow down evaporation.
- To make it easy to top up water levels, bury a seep or perforated hose in the grit layer, with the underground end blocked.
- In a larger bog garden, stepping stones or log sections allow easy access and will prevent the moist soil from becoming compacted as you work around the plants.

PLANTS FOR A DAMP ENVIRONMENT
There are many ordinary perennials and, especially, ferns that will enjoy these moist conditions, but for a wider choice try looking also in the water plant section of nurseries for semi-aquatics such as marsh marigolds (Caltha palustris).

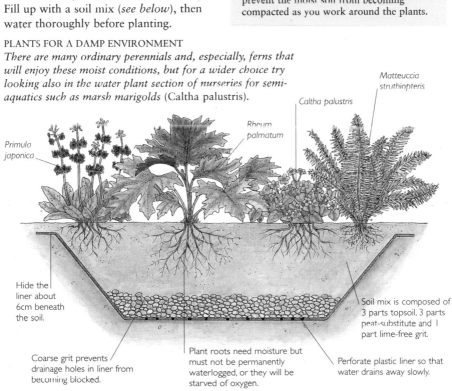

Matteuccia struthiopteris

Caltha palustris

Rheum palmatum

Primula japonica

Hide the liner about 6cm beneath the soil.

Coarse grit prevents drainage holes in liner from becoming blocked.

Plant roots need moisture but must not be permanently waterlogged, or they will be starved of oxygen.

Soil mix is composed of 3 parts topsoil, 3 parts peat-substitute and 1 part lime-free grit.

Perforate plastic liner so that water drains away slowly.

◀ LUXURIANT SCENE *Lush green hostas provide a vibrant foil for pink persicarias.*

PLAN FOR A WATERSIDE PLANTING

This plan is ideal for any modest area of moist soil – for example, beside a garden pool, as here, where the reflection of the plants in the water will enhance the effect considerably. It has been designed to provide a display of colourful flowers from spring until late summer (it is shown here in early summer). The scarlet mimulus in particular is invaluable for its long flowering season, while the variegated hosta adds foliage interest.

PLANTING PLAN

1 3 × *Mimulus cupreus* 'Whitecroft Scarlet' ❀, 30cm apart
2 3 × *Iris sibirica*, 45cm apart
3 2 × *Persicaria bistorta* 'Superba' ❀, 60cm apart
4 1 × *Hosta* 'Shade Fanfare' ❀
5 1 × *Trollius europaeus*
6 3 × *Primula japonica* ❀, 35cm apart

1.5m

2m

Mimulus cupreus 'Whitecroft Scarlet' is rather short-lived but produces a brilliant show of flowers as it spreads along the water's edge.

PRIMULA JAPONICA
One of the candelabra primulas, which make charming poolside plants. Divide congested clumps in late summer when leaves are dying down.

IRIS SIBIRICA
The violet flowers stand up well above the clumps of strap-shaped leaves in summer. There are many types of Siberian iris in different colours to choose from; shades available include good pale blues, yellow, deeper purples, dark red and white.

PLANT CHOICES

Many plants grown on damp ground tend to become very large, so choose carefully if space is limited. Rheums, ligularias, gunneras, *Iris laevigata* and *Rodgersia pinnata* are often shown by poolsides, yet all are very vigorous and will dominate small sites. If you want a lush, leafy look but do not have much space, focus on interesting foliage and warm, vivid flower tones: a variety of ferns, perhaps, interspersed with the rich purple leaves and scarlet flower spikes of the perennial lobelias 'Queen Victoria' or 'Dark Crusader', or the mahogany stems and coppery-pink flowers of the geum 'Leonard's Variety'.

Persicaria bistorta 'Superba' flowers over a long period. It can be invasive but unwanted patches are easily uprooted.

Hosta 'Shade Fanfare' produces a bonus of short spires of lavender-blue, funnel-shaped flowers in summer.

Trollius europaeus produces lemon-yellow, double buttercup-like flowers in early and mid-summer.

PERENNIALS IN CONTAINERS

Many hardy perennials grow happily in containers. For practical reasons, small and medium-sized plants are best, though where a dramatic effect is required, tall plants such as phormiums make excellent focal features. Low, trailing plants can be used to soften pot or tub edges. Remember that foliage colour, texture and shape is highlighted in raised plantings. Evergreens are invaluable, giving pleasure through the year.

CHOOSING THE RIGHT CONTAINER

The choice of container is enormous: glazed bowls and urns, terracotta or plastic pots, traditional timber tubs, and stone sinks. Choose materials that tie in with other hard surfaces in your garden, such as brickwork. If plants are to be in containers for more than one season, they must have room for their roots; small containers also lose moisture too quickly. All plants in containers will need regular watering and occasional repotting. Choose frost-proof materials that will be as hardy as the perennials you plant in them or, if you wish to use more fragile containers for summer display, keep plants in plastic pots within them to minimize root disturbance.

PRACTICAL TIPS

• Before planting, soak new terracotta pots in water overnight to reduce evaporation from the compost through the porous clay.
• A loam-based compost such as John Innes No 3 is best for long-term perennials. Use ericaceous compost for lime-hating plants.
• Keep drainage holes free by raising containers off the ground on blocks or bricks, or use purpose-made terracotta feet.
• Slow-release fertilizer granules keep plants well-fed for about a season – or apply liquid feed at intervals during the growing season.
• Unless you want to group plants with similar needs, such as rock plants, giving plants the right growing conditions is much easier if you use only one plant per container.

Plunge the pot in water

Make sure that drainage holes at the base of the pot are not blocked

Fill two-thirds of the bucket with water

WATERING BEFORE PLANTING
Submerge the plant, still in its pot, in a bucket of water. When bubbles stop appearing the root ball is thoroughly soaked.

PROVIDING GOOD DRAINAGE
Before adding compost, put a shallow layer of drainage material such as terracotta crocks or polystyrene pieces in the base of the container.

◄PINK AND GREEN *Pinks, as in these geranium flowers, look surprisingly good with terracotta.*

PLAN FOR A GROUP OF CONTAINERS

This grouping provides a long season of interest. Early violets and pulsatillas are followed by campanulas and diascias with creeping thyme. These shallow-rooting plants are happy in a trough. Agapanthus provides a tall focal point; geraniums flower all season long, while heucheras give year-round foliage interest. These need deeper pots (here 50cm deep and across at the rim).

PLANTING PLAN

1 1 × *Geranium* × *oxonianum*
2 1 × *Heuchera micrantha* 'Palace Purple'
3 1 × *Thymus serpyllum*
4 1 × *Viola riviniana* Purpurea Group
5 2 × *Diascia* 'Salmon Supreme'
6 3 × *Pulsatilla vulgaris*
7 1 × *Campanula portenschlagiana*
8 2 × *Geranium* × *cantabrigiense* 'Biokovo'
9 3 × *Agapanthus campanulatus* 'Isis'

Geranium × *oxonianum* produces its dainty pink flowers from late spring through until autumn.

Heuchera micrantha 'Palace Purple' bears airy cream flowers followed by rose-pink seedheads.

Thymus serpyllum will creep over the sides of a trough. It has whorls of purple flowers in summer.

VIOLA RIVINIANA
Purplish leaves set off these pale violet flowers. It will readily self-seed into paving cracks around any container.

Diascia 'Salmon Supreme' will flower non-stop from summer to mid-autumn.

ALSO RECOMMENDED FOR CONTAINERS

FLOWERING PLANTS
Dicentra spectabilis 'Alba' ♈
Limonium (statice), especially
  L. platyphyllum 'Violetta'
Osteospermums, especially
  'Stardust'
Primulas: *P. allionii*,
  P. rosea ♈; *P. vulgaris* subsp.
  sibthorpii ♈; *P. denticulata* ♈
Viola cornuta ♈

FOLIAGE PLANTS
Carex flagellifera
Hostas: 'Ginko Craig', 'Ground
  Master', 'Golden Tiara' ♈,
  H. ventricosa ♈
Hakonechloa macra 'Aureola' ♈
Houttuynia cordata
  'Chameleon'
Mentha suaveolens 'Variegata'
Sedum spathulifolium

CREEPING PLANTS
Arabis
Aubrieta
Campanula cochleariifolia
  'Flore Pleno'
Dryas octopetala ♈
Sedum acre 'Aureum'
Sempervivums, especially
  S. arachnoideum subsp.
  tomentosum ♈

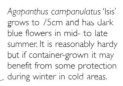

Agapanthus campanulatus 'Isis'
grows to 75cm and has dark
blue flowers in mid- to late
summer. It is reasonably hardy
but if container-grown it may
benefit from some protection
during winter in cold areas.

Geranium x cantabrigiense
'Biokovo' makes a compact
plant, with pinkish-white
flowers in summer

PULSATILLA VULGARIS
These silky spring flowers are
followed by equally delightful
seedheads. It must have sun
and good drainage.

Campanula portenschlagiana is
good for softening the sides of a
trough. Flowers cover the plant in
mid-summer and the leaves are
evergreen. Keep it in check or it
will swamp other plants.

LOOKING AFTER PERENNIALS

GIVING PLANTS A GOOD START

PLANTING AND CARING FOR YOUR perennials can be very rewarding, and the most valuable time you can spend on them is right at the start – choosing the right plants for your soil and site, preparing the ground well, selecting healthy specimens and planting them with care are the key tasks that will repay themselves all through the season with a healthy, vigorous display.

SECRETS OF SUCCESSFUL GARDENING

Garden tasks need not be a burden, and can even be enjoyable. They give you the chance to appreciate your plants at close quarters, and the pleasure of seeing your choices re-emerge, develop, flower and fade during every season of the year.

"Little and often" is the secret to stop garden tasks building up into a lot of work. Find time regularly to take a stroll around your garden or patio inspecting your plants, and you may be able to nip all sorts of problems in the bud immediately, and help your plants look their best. Uprooting weeds as they emerge is not only easier than removing them when large, it also means less disturbance to your plants' roots.

Plant problems are best dealt with before they are able to take a hold: simply picking off a pest or an affected shoot may be enough to stop the problem in its tracks. Regular deadheading improves and extends many plants' flowering display. Water your new plants well, and they shouldn't need it when mature – saving hours of work (and precious water). And if you find staking a chore, choose free-standing perennials that do not need support.

USEFUL PLANT TERMS

- **Crown** Base of a plant, where roots and stems join.
- **Cultivar** Variation on a natural *species* that is selected or bred for a special characteristic. The breeder chooses a name for the plant, for example, *Dicentra* 'Stuart Boothman'.
- **Dormancy** Pause of plant growth and activity, usually during cold winter months.
- **Flowerhead** Mass of small flowers that appear to form a single flower.
- **Genus** Group of plant *species* that share a range of characteristics, such as *Dicentra*.
- **Hybrid** Cross-breed of different *species*, indicated by the symbol '×' in the Latin name.
- **Rhizome** Underground, creeping, thick fleshy stem that sends out roots and shoots.
- **Root ball** Roots and surrounding soil visible when plant is removed from pot.
- **Species** Group of plants that can breed together to produce similar offspring, for example *Dicentra spectabilis*.
- **Subspecies, variety, form** Naturally occurring variations within a *species*, with an additional name in italics following the abbreviations subsp., var. and f. For example, *Dicentra spectabilis* f. *alba*, a white-flowered form of the pink-flowered species.

◀ POPPY APPEAL *In early summer, oriental poppies add a fresh touch to long-flowering euphorbias.*

PREPARING THE GROUND

BEFORE PLANTING PERENNIALS, it is essential to prepare the site thoroughly; once they begin to grow and spread, access to the soil will be much more difficult. If a site has been neglected, your first task will be to remove any perennial weeds. The soil should then be dug over or turned over – a motorized rotavator is a boon where there are large areas of soil – and, unless your soil is very rich, organic materials added to improve soil structure and quality.

CLEARING WEEDS

On new ground that you want to prepare for planting, you must first remove any persistent perennial weeds, such as ground elder and bindweed, either with weedkiller or by conscientious hand-clearing, since their roots spread widely underground and will infest those of your plants. If the site is badly infested, it is well worth spraying the whole area with a systemic weedkiller the season before planting. Other weeds, such as groundsel and dandelions, will lurk in the soil as seeds and spring up throughout the year; they can be hoed off as they appear. Even when you don't have time to hoe, pick off any weed flowerheads you see before they have the chance to set seed.

USING WEEDKILLER

• Always seek advice at your local garden centre before buying and using weedkiller.
• "Contact" weedkiller destroys annual weeds, but only makes the top growth of perennial weeds die down; the roots survive.
• "Systemic" weedkiller destroys foliage, stems and roots of both annual and perennial weeds, without affecting the soil. It is most effective when weeds are in full growth.
• Only use spray systemic weedkiller on areas that are yet to be planted.
• In planted areas, apply spot treatments with a brush so as not to harm other plants.
• Some perennial weeds may need more than one treatment.

REMOVING WEEDS BY HAND
Fork up the weed, holding main stems close to the soil as you lift to help get as much of the root up as possible. Fork over and sift to remove stray pieces of root that will re-shoot.

USING BLACK POLYTHENE
If you can delay planting for a season or two, cover the area with a sheet of thick black plastic to starve weeds of light. Anchor the edges in the soil using a spade.

MAKING DIGGING EASIER

Digging over a large area is much easier if you follow a methodical pattern. Single digging (*see below*) breaks up and aerates soil without bringing the lower, infertile subsoil to the surface. You can also take the opportunity to fork in organic matter in the base of the trenches. Do not dig when the soil is sodden, as this will damage the soil structure. Keep your back straight and take a break as soon as you feel tired.

FIRST TRENCH
Mark out small, manageable areas. Starting in one corner, dig out a trench one spit (spade blade) deep and about 30cm wide. Reserve the soil you remove; this will be used to fill the last trench that you dig.

REMAINING AREA
Working backwards so as not to compact the soil, dig a second trench, turning soil into the first. Bury any annual weeds. Continue until the area is dug, filling the last trench with the soil from the first.

USING A ROTAVATOR

If you are planning to use a rotavator for large, neglected areas, it is essential that you clear the garden of perennial weeds first. Otherwise, the blades will mince up their roots into tiny pieces, each with the potential to regrow and shoot, vastly multiplying the problem. When hiring or buying machinery, for safety's sake, ask for a demonstration first. Wear goggles and keep a firm grip as you work.

IMPROVING YOUR SOIL STRUCTURE

Digging and forking improve the soil structure to some extent, but it can be further improved by the addition of well-rotted organic matter. This will enhance the soil's drainage, aeration, fertility and moisture-holding properties. Adding the material in the season prior to planting will give it time to become well incorporated.

ENRICHING YOUR SOIL
Fork in organic materials such as garden compost, well-rotted manure, composted bark or leafmould. Repeat in subsequent years.

LEVELLING THE SURFACE
Before planting, use a wide-tined rake to break up remaining clods of soil on the surface; this makes weeding much easier.

PLANTING PERENNIALS

M OST PERENNIALS ARE SOLD as container-grown plants, which can be planted at any time of year except in very frosty weather. The traditional times to plant – spring and autumn – are the best, as mild, damp weather helps plants to establish well. Avoid planting in hot, sunny weather because of the difficulty of keeping the plants watered sufficiently. Plants will also suffer a check to growth.

CHOOSING A HEALTHY PLANT

Do not buy perennials showing signs of disease or neglect, such as wilted leaves or a mass of roots appearing out of the bottom of the container. Look for plants with sturdy top growth and thick, strong stems. Do not buy a plant with tangled roots coming out of the base of its pot, or one growing among weeds and moss.

MONEY-SAVING TIP

Do not judge a plant by its size, as an older, bigger one may take a long time to get established. A smaller specimen with good fresh growth will be less expensive and grow away quickly. Once established, it can be divided to produce more plants (*see p.57*).

Strong, healthy top growth with unmarked leaves

Clean, moist compost

Established, vigorous roots

HEALTHY PLANT
This specimen is healthy and weed-free. Other excellent signs include short, stocky growth, lots of shoots and well-developed roots.

Weak, spindly top growth

Moss and weed growing on compost

Old, woody base

BADLY GROWN PLANT
This plant's wasted top growth and signs of moss and weeds growing on the compost indicate lack of care and nourishment.

POT-BOUND PLANT
Never buy plants with roots wound around the inside of the pot. Plants like this are almost impossible to establish successfully.

Pot-bound roots form a tight, congested mass

PLANTING CONTAINER-GROWN PERENNIALS

Never plant in frozen or very dry soil – this usually ends in disaster. Before planting a group of plants, set them out in their pots to find the best arrangement and spacing. Water well before and after planting.

PRACTICAL TIP

To water purchased plants really thoroughly before planting, soak them in their pots in a bucket of water for about 15 minutes.

1 Dig a planting hole twice as wide and to the correct depth *(see below)*. Tap the pot to slide out the plant.

2 Scrape off the top layer of compost with any moss and weeds. Tease out the roots slightly with your fingers.

3 Place the plant in the hole, taking care not to damage the roots. Backfill with soil, firm it well, and water.

PLANTING TO THE CORRECT DEPTH

Plant most perennials, especially if in doubt, at the same depth as in their pots. Some, however, grow better with their crowns above soil level; others shoot more strongly if planted deeper.

Crown is slightly above the ground

Crown is at ground level

Crown is about 2cm below ground level

Crown is about 10cm below the surface

SHALLOW PLANTING *Recommended for* Sisyrinchium striatum, *pinks* (Dianthus), *milkweed* (Asclepias), *rheums, phormiums and irises.*

GROUND LEVEL *Most perennials should be planted at ground level. If planted too deeply, the base of the stems will be prone to rot.*

BELOW GROUND *Recommended for hostas, dicentras, foxtail lilies* (Eremurus), *peonies and lily-of-the-valley* (Convallaria).

DEEP PLANTING *Recommended for Solomon's seal* (Polygonatum), *crinum, monkshood* (Aconitum), *crocosmias and alstroemerias.*

PLANT CARE THROUGH THE YEAR

GOOD PREPARATION and planting encourage plants to make healthy, sustained growth. Water only until established, preferably using recycled water or collected rainwater. Mulching helps to suppress weeds, conserve moisture and improve soil structure. Some perennials may need support; many can be encouraged to flower better, and some benefit from regular division (*overleaf*).

FEEDING AND WATERING

An annual application of bonemeal or general-purpose granular fertilizer in spring should provide a sufficient supply of nutrients. Keep all fertilizers off leaves, flowers and stems, to avoid scorching.

The need for watering will depend on soil and weather conditions, and on the nature of the individual plants. Most established perennials grown on well-cultivated ground will need little watering (many positively thrive in dry soil), but young plants must have plenty of moisture until they are well established. To achieve maximum benefit, irrigate in early evening when the water will evaporate less quickly, and direct the water down to the roots.

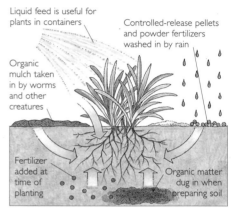

Liquid feed is useful for plants in containers

Controlled-release pellets and powder fertilizers washed in by rain

Organic mulch taken in by worms and other creatures

Fertilizer added at time of planting

Organic matter dug in when preparing soil

WAYS OF FEEDING PLANTS
A careful balance of organic matter, fertilizers and water will ensure healthy plant growth.

APPLYING DIFFERENT TYPES OF MULCH

Organic mulches help to suppress weed growth, retain moisture and, as they are gradually incorporated into the ground, will help to improve soil structure.

Proprietary mulching sheets made of paper or geotextile let water through yet make effective weed suppressors. Apply mulches in spring or summer, when the soil is moist.

ORGANIC MULCH
Apply compost, rotted manure or leafmould at least 3cm deep. It can scorch stems so leave the base of plants clear.

MULCHING SHEETS
Special garden textile may be used as a mulch if laid before planting. Cut crosses in the textile to plant through.

ORNAMENTAL MULCH
Shredded bark or stone chips hide mulching sheets or provide a decorative, weed-suppressant soil covering.

Providing Plants with Support

Start with as many free-standing plants as possible (*see below*) to avoid the need for staking. Support is necessary for tall perennials, or for plants with fragile stems, especially in exposed areas. Insert supports early in the season – this will make the task easier and minimize damage to growth. Use canes that are about two-thirds of the plant's eventual height, and push them firmly but carefully into the ground near the base of the shoots. Space canes evenly around the edge of clumps. Cane guards such as corks are recommended to prevent accidental eye injury. Although obtrusive at first, ring or link stakes will soon be camouflaged by foliage.

RING OF CANES
Place canes around multi-stemmed perennials or plants with a floppy growth habit. Loop twine around the circle to support the plant.

LINK STAKES
Support tall clumps with link stakes. Insert these deep into the ground at the start of the growing season, raising them as the plant gains height.

RING STAKES
Ring stakes support clump-forming perennials. Insert the stakes deeply, then raise them as the plant grows through the support.

SINGLE CANE
Delphiniums and other plants with tall single stems should be staked when 20–25cm high. Use garden twine to tie the stem loosely to the cane.

WHICH PLANTS NEED SUPPORT?

FREE-STANDING PERENNIALS
Many clump-forming perennials, including aquilegias, cimicifugas, daylilies (*Hemerocallis*), hardy geraniums, geums and rudbeckias, do not need support. Look for (often newer) short or compact versions of slender-stemmed plants such as delphiniums and asters to cut down the need for staking.

STAKING SINGLE STEMS
Stake individual stems of monkshood (*Aconitum*), campanulas, delphiniums, sea hollies (*Eryngium*), physostegias and verbascums.

SUPPORTING CLUMPS
Tall clumps such as astilbes, goldenrod (*Solidago*), heleniums, tall asters and liatris may need encircling support, such as twine around canes or link stakes (*see above*); perennials with heavy flowerheads, such as dahlias, lupins and peonies, will benefit from the extra support of ring stakes.

AQUILEGIA

IMPROVING FOLIAGE AND FLOWERING DISPLAYS

Thinning or pinching out shoots results in better flowers on certain plants. For many more, deadheading and cutting back can extend the flowering season and will prevent the plants from self-seeding. The amount of stem to be removed depends on the plant. These tasks are by no means essential, but do result in a finer show.

BETTER FLOWERS
In spring, thin young shoots when no more than a third of their final height. Remove about one shoot in three by cutting or pinching out the weakest at the base.

BUSHY PLANTS
When the shoots are one–third of their final height, "stop" or pinch out the top 2.5–5cm, just above a leaf joint. This encourages branching and bushier growth.

Plants improved by thinning:
Phlox, Michaelmas daisies (*Aster*), Lupins, Delphiniums, Golden rod (*Solidago*)

Plants improved by pinching out:
Michaelmas daisies, Chrysanthemums (stop twice), Heleniums, Phlox, Rudbeckias

MORE FLOWERS
Remove flowerheads as they start to fade, cutting the stem back to a sideshoot (if possible). This will encourage the plant to produce another flush of flowers.

NEW GROWTH
Cut back old flowered stems to ground level as new shoots begin to grow from the base. This may produce a second display of flowers later in the season.

Plants that benefit from deadheading:
Chrysanthemums, Dianthus, Lupins Mimulus, Penstemons, Phlox

Plants that regrow well if cut back:
Anthemis, Catmints (*Nepeta*), Centaureas, Delphiniums, Geraniums, Salvias

CLEARING AWAY TATTY GROWTH

When plants have finished their display, you can begin tidying up. Remove weeds and cut down decaying foliage and dead stems to the base. Mark the position of each plant by inserting a label in the soil. Attractive stems and seedheads (*pp.17–19*) can be left for winter, but try to tidy up before vulnerable new shoots appear.

▶ CUTTING BACK BEFORE WINTER
Cut stems to ground level. Insert labels (see inset) to avoid accidentally digging over the plant while the soil is bare.

DIVIDING CLUMP-FORMING PERENNIALS

Division is the most reliable way of maintaining plant health and increasing stock. Most vigorous perennials (such as this sedum) will benefit from division every three to five years. Divide clumps at any time (except in frosty weather) from late autumn to spring, when they will be able to re-establish successfully. Keep only the healthiest, newest sections for replanting.

PRACTICAL TIPS

• Divide spring-flowering plants in autumn, and late summer/autumn bloomers in spring.
• For healthy, vigorous phlox and asters, divide established plants every year.
• A short, sharp garden knife is useful for dividing tough plant crowns.
• Water in all replanted pieces well.

Holding the roots, firmly pull the plant apart with your hands, if possible

1 Lift the clump by pushing a fork well under the rootball. Carefully loosen the roots by levering it up and down. Shake off surplus soil, or wash off with a hose.

2 Divide the clump into smaller pieces by hand or with a knife. Discard old, woody parts of the plant, replanting only vigorous portions of root with several new shoots.

DIVIDING IRISES AND BERGENIAS

Divide plants with fleshy rhizomes near the surface, such as bearded irises and bergenias, by splitting the clump into pieces by hand (for old plants you may need to undercut the clump with a spade). Cut the rhizomes into sections with a sharp knife. Plant only young sections, half-burying the rhizomes and keeping the leaves and buds upright.

1 Having lifted the plant, use your hands or a small knife to split the clump into manageable pieces.

2 Using a sharp knife, detach firm, young rhizomes, each with a shoot, discarding old, woody parts.

Trim the foliage (cut iris leaves back to about 15cm). Plant shallowly, firm in well and water thoroughly.

RAISING NEW PLANTS

THE MAIN WAYS OF PROPAGATING PLANTS are by division (*see pp.56–57*), taking cuttings and sowing seed (*see p.61*). Only division and cuttings will produce plants identical to the parent, important for named cultivars. It helps to have a cold frame but a light windowsill can suffice. A sharp knife or blade is essential.

TAKING STEM TIP CUTTINGS

A tip cutting is taken from the top of a stem just below a leaf joint. A cutting must have at least one leaf joint to root. Make sure the stem is clean before inserting into cuttings compost (half sand, half peat or peat substitute), rather than garden soil. Keep the compost moist and, during the dry season, continue watering when the cuttings have rooted. The best time to take cuttings is in spring.

1 **Select a short length of stem** about 7–12cm long from the tip of a healthy, non-flowering shoot. Using a sharp pair of secateurs or garden scissors, make the cut.

Leaf joint

STEM TIP CUTTING

2 **Trim the lower end** just below a leaf joint using a sharp knife or secateurs, reducing its length to 5–7cm. Remove the lower leaves to expose 2–3cm of stem at the base.

3 **Insert the cuttings** (usually 5–6) around the edge of a 7 or 10cm pot filled with cuttings compost. Water, label, and cover with a plastic bag supported by canes to keep condensation off the cuttings. Place out of direct sunlight.

Potting compost

STEM TIP CUTTINGS

SUITABLE PLANTS:

Asters
Catmint (*Nepeta*)
Diascias
Oenothera macrocarpa
Penstemons

Perennial wallflowers (*Erysimum*)
Persicarias
Pinks (*Dianthus*)
Salvias, some
Violas

4 **When the cuttings** have rooted (tap out the pot and look from after about 3 weeks), lift and pot them singly. Water in and shade them until growing well.

TAKING BASAL STEM CUTTINGS

This technique is used for perennials that produce clusters of new shoots at the base in spring. Cuttings from plants with hollow or pithy stems, such as delphiniums and lupins, as well as from plants with soft, solid stems, such as catmint (*Nepeta*) and phlox, can be rooted successfully if taken from healthy plants in mid-spring.

Leaf joint (node)

BASAL CUTTING

1 **Take cuttings** when the new shoots are 3.5–5cm high. Using a sharp knife, cut as close to the base as possible so that part of the woody, basal tissue is included in the cutting.

2 **Remove the lower leaves** of the cutting so that at least one node is clearly visible. Trim the lower end, making a straight, clean cut, and remove any soil from the cutting.

3 **Insert the cuttings** into a pot of cuttings compost. Firm, water, and let the compost drain. Label and put the pot in a cold frame or place it on a windowsill out of direct sunlight. Cover with a plastic bag.

Insert cuttings so that the first leaf stalks are above compost level

4 **When rooted,** lift and separate the cuttings, retaining some compost around roots. Pot individually and grow on in a cold frame or sheltered spot; plant in autumn if well-grown, or wait until next spring.

BASAL CUTTINGS

SUITABLE PLANTS:
Achilleas
Anaphalis
Anthemis tinctoria
Campanulas
Catmint *(Nepeta)*
Chelone obliqua
Chrysanthemums
Delphiniums
False mallow *(Sidalcea)*
Goat's rue *(Galega)*
Heliopsis
Loosestrife *(Lysimachia)*
Lupins
Lychnis
Obedient plant *(Physostegia virginiana)*
Phlox
Tanacetum coccineum
Veronicas
Willowherb *(Epilobium)*

How to Propagate by Root Cuttings

Root cuttings can be taken in winter from some perennials with thick roots such as verbascums, phlox and acanthus. It is essential to plant the cutting the right way up – making differently angled cuts will help you identify the top and bottom.

ALTERNATIVE METHOD

For thin-rooted perennials (*see box below*), lay the cuttings horizontally on moist, firmed compost. Cover with a layer of compost.

1 **Lift the plant** and wash the roots. Choose pencil-thick roots and cut them close to the crown. Keep all the cuttings the right way up.

2 **Trim the roots** smooth and cut into lengths of 5–10cm. Make a straight cut at the upper end and an angled cut at the lower end.

3 **Fill a pot** with cuttings compost. Using a dibber, insert the cuttings, straight end at the top, flush with the surface. Firm and water in.

4 **Top-dress the pots** with coarse grit and label. Place in a cold frame or in a sheltered spot with some protective cover. Do not water until the cuttings start to shoot.

5 **When the cuttings** have developed shoots, lift and pot up individually, using loam-based compost. Water, label and return to the cold frame until large enough to plant out.

ROOT CUTTINGS

SUITABLE PLANTS:

Acanthus	Echinacea	Japanese anemones	Peonies
Brunnera	Echinops	(lay horizontally)	*Primula denticulata*
Campanulas	Eryngiums	Oriental poppies	Pulmonarias
(lay horizontally)	Filipendula	Phlox	Verbascums

GROWING PERENNIALS FROM SEED

Simple and inexpensive, raising plants from seed, especially when collected yourself, is ideal when lots of plants are required. Few cultivars, however, breed true and species may vary from the norm. It usually takes a full year to produce a flowering plant.

SAVING SEED

Save your own seed from perennials such as aquilegias, astrantias, campanulas, Jacob's ladder (*Polemonium*) and scabious.

1 **Fill a tray** with moist multi-purpose or seed compost. Level it with a block of wood and firm to about 1cm below the rim.

2 **Sprinkle the seed** over as evenly as possible. Cover with a fine layer of sieved compost. Water gently, without dislodging the seed.

3 **Cover the tray** with a sheet of glass or plastic to retain moisture. Put in a cold frame or sheltered place, out of direct sunlight.

4 **When the seedlings** have developed two pairs of leaves, transfer them into small pots. Handle seedlings by their seed leaves (the lowest pair), as stems are easily damaged. Grow them on in a sheltered place out of direct sunlight, in a cold frame if possible, until large enough to plant out.

Use a dibber to make the hole

LAYERING PINKS

A few plants, most notably carnations and pinks (*Dianthus*), can be propagated by layering. Mix some peat substitute and sharp sand into the soil around the plant. Remove all but the top 4–5 pairs of leaves on some non-flowering shoots (*as right*). Using a small, sharp knife, cut a tongue in each stem just below the lowest leaves, slicing through a leaf joint (*see inset*). Insert the cut stems into the prepared soil and pin down with a thin piece of wire. Keep the area moist until roots have formed (about 5–6 weeks), then lift the rooted layers and pot or plant out.

How to Avoid Plant Problems

PREVENTATIVE RATHER THAN REMEDIAL action will minimize the risk of pest and disease problems. A healthy plant is far less likely to succumb to attack, so start with good, vigorous stock and care for it well. Good garden management is essential, and the encouragement of beneficial insects and hand-picking of pests and diseased leaves will help. It is preferable not to use garden chemicals, which may kill indiscriminately and also often become ineffective after a while.

Creating a Healthy Garden

Good cultivation techniques, clean tools and the inclusion of trouble-free plants (such as alchemillas, anemones, artemisias, campanulas, doronicums, geraniums, geums, lobelias, phlomis and stachys) will do a lot to avoid pests and diseases. Always keep beds and borders tidy; weeds can be a jumping-off point for pests and diseases. If you compost, remember not to add any diseased or infested material. Pick off pests and diseased leaves regularly to prevent the

problem invading the healthy parts of the plant. Grow plants such as *Anemone* × *hybrida*, campanulas and rudbeckias, which will encourage beneficial wildlife: centipedes feed on many soil pests, ladybirds and their larvae feed on pests such as aphids (*see below*), while spiders trap a range of pests in their webs. Use chemicals only when absolutely necessary, and always ask your local garden centre to recommend a suitable product.

VINE WEEVILS
Before making a purchase, and again before planting, inspect plants to find and destroy any adult vine weevils on the foliage or larvae in the soil or compost.

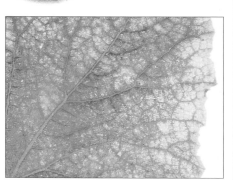

RED SPIDER MITE
Most commonly a greenhouse pest, red spider mite is encouraged in the garden by hot, dry summers. Conserving moisture helps deter it.

APHIDS
Aphids pierce stems with their mouth parts, sucking out sap; they literally sap a plant's strength. They can also spread diseases.

A CALENDAR OF SEASONAL REMINDERS

SPRING

• Clear away any debris and remove weeds. Do not compost perennial weeds or any plant material showing signs of pests and diseases.

• Prepare soil for planting if you have not already done so. Any manure added now must be very well-rotted.

• Buy healthy plants with sturdy growth; mulch around them when planted and water them regularly.

• Feed plants with a general fertilizer such as blood, fish and bone or bonemeal.

• Stake plants that need it: be careful not to damage new growth.

• Divide or thin any overcrowded plants.

• You can take cuttings of many perennials, but they need shelter in a propagator, greenhouse or cold frame while the weather is still chilly.

• In mild springs aphids may multiply before populations of their predators, such as ladybirds, can build up. If infestations are bad, consider using an aphid-specific insecticide, or spray with insecticidal soap.

• Sow hardy annuals to fill gaps between perennials.

SUMMER

• Pull up link and ring stakes carefully as plants gain height and tie in tall stems to cane supports.

• Water new plants before they show signs of stress due to drought.

• Apply more mulch, if necessary, to conserve moisture.

• Water plants in containers regularly, and give a liquid feed to those not supplied with slow-release fertilizer granules.

• If plants are lost to drought, consider drought-loving replacements such as aubretias, coreopsis, dianthus and oenotheras.

• Cut back faded flowerheads unless you want plants to self-seed. If you wish to collect seed, leave just a few seedheads on the plant.

• Weed regularly, and keep an eye out for signs of pests and diseases.

• In dry summers, plants prone to mildew, such as phlox and asters, are especially vulnerable. Pick off leaves showing a grey-white fungal bloom. Consider spraying badly affected plants.

• Keep any cuttings you take well watered and shaded from hot sun.

AUTUMN

• Weed thoroughly.

• Plant perennials that you wish to flower in spring.

• Lift and divide overcrowded clumps of perennials.

• While the weather is still mild, autumn is an excellent time for planting perennials in well-prepared ground. Do not buy plants now, however, that like sun and light, free-draining soil: they may suffer badly from winter wet when young and are best planted in spring.

• Check plants regularly for signs of pests and diseases: slugs and snails may become a problem again as the weather becomes cooler and wetter.

• Tidy beds and borders as plants fade, cutting down and removing dead stems and foliage. This will also ensure that late-flowering perennials are shown off at their best.

WINTER

• Tidy up beds and borders, cutting down and removing dead growth. Insert labels where plants have died down completely, so you know where they are.

• Lift and destroy plants that have succumbed to disease.

• You can take root cuttings of many perennials now, but they need shelter from cold.

• Move perennials in containers to a sheltered spot.

• Prepare bare areas of soil for planting in spring, adding plenty of organic matter such as garden compost or a purchased equivalent, well-rotted manure or leafmould. Time and the action of frosts will help these materials break down and become well incorporated into your soil, improving its texture.

ORIENTAL POPPY

RECOMMENDED PERENNIALS

THE RANGE OF PERENNIALS here have symbols that indicate their preferred conditions, but many are not unduly demanding. Nearly all are completely hardy; a few borderline plants may need protection from severe cold. More tips on care and propagation may be found in *Looking After Perennials (pp.49–63)*.

◘ *Prefers full sun* ◙ *Prefers partial shade* ▦ *Tolerates full shade* ◊ *Prefers well-drained soil* ◊ *Prefers moist soil* ❋❋❋ *Fully hardy (down to -15°C)* ❋❋ *Frost hardy (down to -5°C)* **Tall** *Over 1.2m* **Medium** *60cm–1.2m* **Small** *up to 60cm* ♀*RHS Award of Garden Merit*

A

Acanthus (Bear's breeches)
Tall, architectural plant, with large, deeply cut leaves. Sturdy white and mauve flower spikes, borne in late summer, are useful for dried winter decoration. Divide or sow seed in spring, or take root cuttings in winter.
◘ ◊ ❋❋❋
A. mollis p.34. Also recommended: *A. spinosus* ♀

Achillea
Forms medium-height clumps of feathery foliage. Dense, flat flowerheads appear in summer, long-lasting and good for drying. Divide or take basal stem cuttings in spring; sow seed in late spring or early summer.
◘ ◊ ❋❋❋
A. filipendula 'Gold Plate' ♀ *p.30.* Also recommended: *A.* 'Coronation Gold' ♀ *A.* 'Moonshine' ♀

ACONITUM CARMICHAELII 'ARENDSII'

Aconitum (Monkshood)
Tall spires of hooded flowers in indigo blue, white or yellow are borne in summer. Divide the tuberous roots every two years, in autumn or winter, to encourage strong stems. Sow seed in autumn. All parts are toxic.
◘ ◊ ❋❋❋
Recommended: *A. carmichaelii* 'Arendsii', *A.* 'Spark's Variety' ♀

Agapanthus
Small-to-medium plants with erect stems, topped by round heads of blue or white tubular flowers in late summer. Strap-shaped leaves. Divide in spring. In cold areas, protect crowns with straw in winter.
◘ ◊ ❋❋
A. campanulatus p.47.

Ajuga (Bugle)
Semi- or fully evergreen low, spreading plants, ideal for ground cover. Some have purple or variegated foliage; all bear short flower spikes in spring/early summer. Make new plants by digging up rooted stems in early summer.
◘ ◊ ❋❋❋

Alchemilla mollis ♀
(Lady's mantle)
Small to medium-sized, ground-cover plant with soft, circular leaves and masses of tiny, greenish-yellow flowers in summer. Self-sows freely.
◘ ◊ ❋❋❋

◄ SPIRES AND STRIPES *Foxgloves mix with spiky sisyrinchiums and a striped lamium.*

Anemone

Wide range of tuberous or herbaceous perennials bearing cup-shaped flowers in white, blue, pink or red. The tuberous types are often small and flower in spring; the tall, herbaceous, clump-forming Japanese anemones, such as *A. hupehensis*, flower in autumn. All anemones can be divided in autumn.

🔲 ◊ ❀❀❀
A. hupehensis 'Hadspen Abundance' ❦ *p.17*. Also recommended: *A.* × *hybrida* 'Honorine Jobert' ❦

Anthemis

Carpeting or clump-forming plants with a profuse summer crop of yellow or white daisy-like flowers. The ferny foliage is sometimes evergreen. Can be short-lived. Divide in spring or take basal stem cuttings in spring or summer.

🔲 ◊ ❀❀❀
A. punctata subsp. *cupaniana* ❦ *p.28*. Also recommended: *A. tinctoria* 'E.C. Buxton'.

Aquilegia (Columbine)

Erect, small-to-medium height stems bear single and double nodding flowers in late spring and summer in many colours. Sow seed in autumn or spring. Often self-seeds.

🔲 ◊ ❀❀❀
A. vulgaris p.35.

Artemisia

The perennials are bushy, medium-sized evergreen or semi-evergreen foliage plants. The grey or silver fern-like leaves are often aromatic. Cut back foliage in spring. Divide in spring or autumn.

🔲 ◊ ❀❀❀
Recommended: *A. alba* 'Canescens' ❦, *A. ludoviciana* 'Silver Queen' ❦ (can spread).

Aruncus (Goat's beard)

Tall plumes of tiny white flowers are borne in summer above broad hummocks of fern-like foliage. Divide in spring or autumn.

🔲 ◊ ❀❀❀

Aster

Perennials of small-to-medium height, with daisy-flowers. Taller ones may need staking. Sprays of small blue, violet, purple, pink or white flowers mostly appear in late summer

ASTILBE 'APHRODITE'

and autumn and are good for cutting. Take cuttings in spring, or divide in spring or autumn.

🔲 ◊ ❀❀❀
A. × *frikartii* 'Mönch' ❦ *p.29*; *A. novae-belgii* 'Little Pink Beauty' *p.28*. Also recommended: *A. amellus* 'King George' ❦

Astilbe

Small-to-medium plants, with dense clumps of ferny foliage. Numerous red, pink or white flower plumes appear in summer, which last well when cut; dried flowerheads look attractive in winter. Can be used in waterside plantings Divide in spring or autumn.

🔲 ◊ ❀❀❀

Astrantia (Masterwort)

Bears unusual flowers, with pink, white and green papery bracts, in summer and autumn. They lend themselves to cutting and drying. Good ground cover of medium height, suitable for informal planting. Divide in spring, or sow seed in late summer.

🔲 ◊ ❀❀❀
Recommended: *A. major* 'Shaggy' ❦, *A. maxima* ❦

AQUILEGIA 'MUNSTEAD WHITE'

B

Baptisia australis ♀ (False indigo)
Upright, deep-rooted plant of medium height with attractive, divided, blue-green leaves. In summer it bears erect, open spikes of small, pea-like, indigo flowers. Divide or sow seed in spring.
🔲 ◊ ✳✳✳

Bergenia
Low-growing, clump-forming evergreen, valuable for its large glossy leaves, which often turn red in winter. Small, bell-shaped, crimson, pink or white flowers are borne in clusters in late winter and spring. Divide the fleshy roots after flowering.
🔲 ◊ ✳✳✳
B. 'Silberlicht' ♀ *p.38*;
B. 'Baby Doll' *p.28*.

Brunnera
Small perennials producing open clusters of blue forget-me-not-like flowers in early spring. Leaves are large and heart-shaped. Some, such as 'Hadspen Cream' ♀, have variegated foliage that needs protection from wind. Divide in spring, or take root cuttings in mid- to late autumn.
🔲 ◊ ✳✳✳
B. macrophylla ♀ *p.38*.

Buphthalmum salicifolium
Small-to-medium, upright plant producing yellow, daisy-like flowers in summer. Suitable for a wild garden but can be invasive. Divide in spring, or sow seed in late spring or early summer.
🔲 ◊ ✳✳✳

CAMPANULA LATIFOLIA

C

Campanula (Bellflower)
Versatile range of perennials, including small rock plants and tall border species. Blue, pink or white bell- or chalice-shaped flowers, sometimes double, are borne in summer. Leaves are often evergreen, especially if they form basal rosettes. Sow seed or take basal stem cuttings in spring, or divide in spring or autumn.
🔲 ◊ ✳✳✳
C. glomerata 'Purple Pixie' *p.29*; *C. latifolia p.39*; *C. latiloba p.32*; *C. portenschlagiana* ♀ *p.47*.
Also recommended:
C. lactiflora 'Loddon Anna' ♀, *C. persicifolia* 'Fleur de Neige' ♀

Centranthus (Valerian)
Fleshy-leaved plant of medium height, bearing branching heads of small, red, pink or white star-shaped flowers from late spring until autumn. Sow seed in spring or autumn. Self-seeds readily, and tolerates poor conditions.
🔲 ◊ ✳✳✳

Chrysanthemum
Useful autumn flowers that come in a wide range of colours and shapes. Spray and pompon chrysanthemums and those from the Rubellum Group make good perennials for the garden. Take basal stem cuttings in spring, or divide in early spring.
🔲 ◊ ✳✳✳

Cimicifuga (Bugbane)
Tall, upright plant bearing slender spikes of tiny, tufted white flowers in autumn. Attractively divided leaves are mahogany-coloured in some bugbanes. Divide or sow seed in spring.
🔲 ◊ ✳✳✳
Recommended: *C. racemosa* ♀, *C. simplex*.

Convallaria majalis (Lily-of-the-valley)
Low-growing, with narrow, sometimes variegated, leaves. Small, fragrant, waxy white (occasionally pink) bells are borne in spring and early summer. Good for a shady, informal border. Divide in spring or autumn.
🔲 ◊ ✳✳✳

CIMICIFUGA SIMPLEX 'BRUNETTE'

COREOPSIS GRANDIFLORA
'BADENGOLD'

Coreopsis
Small-to-medium bushy plants bearing a profusion of yellow daisy-like flowers in summer that are good for cutting. Divide or sow seed in spring.
▣ ◊ ✳✳✳
Recommended: *C. grandiflora*, *C. verticillata* 'Moonbeam'.

Corydalis
Small, low-growing perennials with tuberous or fleshy roots and fern-like foliage that dies down after flowering. Snapdragon-like blue, pinkish-purple, yellow or white flowers appear in spring. Can make good ground cover. Divide after flowering, or sow seed as soon as it ripens.
▣▣ ◊ ✳✳✳
Recommended: *C. flexuosa* 'China Blue', *C. solida* ♀

Crambe cordifolia
Tall, vigorous plant with long woody roots and big, heart-shaped leaves. Small, white, fragrant flowers are borne in billowing sprays in summer. Divide in spring, or sow seed in spring or autumn.
▣ ◊ ✳✳✳

Crocosmia
Colourful medium-to-tall plants with lance-shaped leaves. Fiery red, orange or yellow flower spikes appear in late summer and early autumn. Flowers are ideal for cutting. Divide in spring.
▣ ◊ ✳✳✳
C. × *crocosmiiflora* 'Emily McKenzie' *p.22*;
C. 'Lucifer' ♀ *p.29*.

Cynara (Cardoon)
Tall, architectural plant bearing large, purple, thistle-like flowerheads in late summer. Long, silver-grey leaves are deeply divided and make broad clumps. Divide plants or sow seed in spring.
▣ ◊ ✳✳✳

D

Delphinium
Classic herbaceous perennials. Plants can range from small to tall; the large hybrids are invaluable in summer for the back of a border. Spikes of single to fully double flowers come in shades of cream, white, lilac-pink or blue, often with a differently coloured, usually dark, central eye or "bee". The spires need individual staking from an early stage. Take basal stem cuttings or sow seed in spring.
▣ ◊ ✳✳✳

DELPHINIUM 'BLUE NILE'

DIANTHUS 'DAD'S FAVOURITE'

Dianthus (Border carnations, pinks)
Huge range of small plants with fragrant summer flowers, mainly in pinks, reds and white, often bicoloured. Tufted foliage is often grey-green. Make new plants by layering, or stem tip cuttings.
▣ ◊ ✳✳✳
D. 'Mrs Sinkins' *p.30*.

Diascia
Small, mat-forming plants bearing upright flower spikes in shades of pink throughout summer. Sow seed in spring; take stem tip cuttings in spring or summer.
▣ ◊ ✳✳
D. 'Salmon Supreme' *p.46*.
Also recommended:
D. rigescens ♀, *D. vigilis* ♀

Dicentra (Bleeding heart)
Small-to-medium plants, with green or grey-green, fern-like foliage. Sprays of heart-shaped, red, pink and white flowers appear in spring. Divide in late winter.
▣ ◊◊ ✳✳✳
D. spectabilis ♀ *p.39*. Also recommended: *D.* 'Luxuriant', *D.* 'Stuart Boothman'.

Dictamnus albus ♀
(Burning bush)
Upright plant of medium
height, with aromatic foliage.
Heads of fragrant, white star-
shaped flowers are borne in
summer. There is a pinkish-
purple variety. Resents
disturbance after planting.
Sow seed as soon as it ripens;
germination is slow.
◨ ◊ ✳✳✳

Digitalis (Foxglove)
There are several biennial or
perennial foxgloves bearing
medium-to-tall spikes of pink,
pale golden-brown or lemon
flowers in summer. Rosettes
of leaves sometimes last over
winter. Divide in spring, or
sow seed in spring or autumn.
◨◨ ◊ ✳✳✳
D. grandiflora ♀ *p.39*. Also
recommended: *D. ferruginea,
D. × mertonensis* ♀

Doronicum 'Miss Mason' ♀
Small, easily-grown plant (*see
p.29*) bearing yellow daisy
flowers in mid- to late spring.
These are good for cutting.
Sow seed in spring, or divide
in autumn.
◨ ◊ ✳✳✳

DIGITALIS FERRUGINEA

ECHINACEA PURPUREA
'ROBERT BLOOM'

E

Echinacea (Coneflower)
Upright, vigorous medium-
height plants, bearing large,
daisy-like, red, pink or white
flowers, with domed centres,
in summer. Sow seed in spring,
take root cuttings in autumn
and winter, or divide in spring
or autumn.
◨ ◊ ✳✳✳

Echinops (Globe thistle)
Medium-to-tall, clump-
forming plants, bearing silver,
grey or blue spherical
flowerheads in summer above
spiny, downy leaves. The
flowers dry well. Sow seed in
spring, divide in autumn or
take root cuttings in winter.
◨ ◊ ✳✳✳
E. bannaticus p.31.

Epilobium (Willowherb)
Willowherbs can be invasive.
E. angustifolium 'Album',
with medium-height spires of
white flowers in summer, is
good in a wild garden. Divide
in spring or autumn.
◨ ◊ ✳✳✳

Epimedium
Small, clump-forming,
deciduous or evergreen plants,
often with coppery leaves.
Dainty white, yellow, pink or
purple flowers appear in
spring. Clip back old foliage
in early spring for the best
display. Good ground cover.
Divide in spring or autumn.
◨ ◊ ✳✳✳
Recommended:
E. grandiflorum ♀, *E. ×
perralchicum* ♀, *E. ×
rubrum* ♀, *E. × youngianum.*

Eryngium (Sea holly)
Thistle-like, medium or tall
plants. Round or egg-shaped,
blue or white flowerheads are
borne in summer above spiky
bracts. Excellent for drying.
Divide in spring, or take root
cuttings in winter.
◨ ◊ ✳✳✳
Recommended: *E. alpinum* ♀,
E. × tripartitum ♀

Eupatorium purpureum
Tall, robust plant, bearing
clusters of small white, pink
or purple flowers from late
summer to autumn. Attracts
bees and butterflies. Foliage
sometimes tinted purple.
◨ ◊ ✳✳✳

Euphorbia (Spurge)
There are several perennial
spurges, varying greatly in
size. Most have eye-catching
yellow-green, occasionally
flame-coloured, flowerheads
in spring and summer. Foliage
is often blue-green. Sow seed
or divide in autumn, take
basal cuttings in spring or
summer. Sap can irritate skin.
◨ ◊ ✳✳✳
Recommended: *E. griffithii,
E. myrsinites* ♀, *E. palustris* ♀,
E. polychroma ♀

EASY FERNS

Athyrium
Medium-sized, deciduous, with lacy fronds, usually green but in *A. niponicum* var. *pictum* ♀ with grey and purple tones.

✳ ◊ ✾✾✾

Dryopteris
Handsome, medium-sized ferns with fronds that form shuttlecocks. Usually deciduous.

✳ ◊ ✾✾✾

Recommended: *D. affinis* ♀, *D. wallichiana* ♀

Matteuccia struthiopteris
Deciduous, spreading fern with tall shuttlecocks of light green fronds.

✳ ◊ ✾✾✾

Polystichum
Mostly evergreen, medium-sized, architectural ferns with fronds fanning out in an open shuttlecock.

✳ ◊ ✾✾✾

Recommended:
P. aculeatum ♀,
P. setiferum ♀

DRYOPTERIS AFFINIS

F

Filipendula (Meadowsweet)
Tall, upright plants bearing plumes of tiny, fragrant, cream or pink flowers from late spring to late summer. Large, lobed leaves are green or gold. Divide in spring or autumn, take root cuttings in late winter or early spring.

▣ ◊ ✾✾✾

Recommended: *F. purpurea* ♀, *F. ulmaria* 'Aurea' ♀

G

Gaillardia
Medium-sized plants with bright, daisy-like, red, orange or yellow flowers borne on slender but sturdy stems over long periods in summer. Cut flowers last well. Plants can be short-lived. Sow seed or divide in spring.

▣ ◊ ✾✾✾

Galega (Goat's rue)
Tall plants producing spires of pea-like, white, blue, mauve or bicoloured flowers from mid-summer. Good for

GAILLARDIA 'DAZZLER'

naturalizing and growing in informal borders. Self-seeds and can be invasive. Divide in spring or late autumn.

▣ ◊◊ ✾✾✾

Geranium (Cranesbill)
Useful and easy perennials of varying sizes. Many make good ground cover. Saucer-to-star-shaped white, pink, purple or blue flowers appear from early to late summer. Lobed leaves are also often attractive. Cut back after flowering to encourage fresh foliage and flowers. Divide or take basal cuttings in spring.

▣▣ ◊ ✾✾✾

G. pratense 'Plenum Caeruleum' *p.34*;
G. × *cantabrigiense* 'Biokovo' *p.47*; *G.* × *oxonianum p.46*. Also recommended:
G. endressii ♀, *G.* 'Johnson's Blue' ♀, *G. macrorrhizum*,
G. × *magnificum* ♀, *G. psilostemon* ♀

Geum
Small, colourful plants for the front of the border with yellow, orange or red flowers from late spring to summer. There are several to choose from; some small species are grown as rock plants. Divide in autumn or spring.

▣ ◊ ✾✾✾

Gypsophila
Airy clouds of tiny white or pink flowers are borne on small- to medium-sized plants from mid-summer. Will trail over banks or walls. Good as cut or dried flowers. There are also some rock garden species. Sow seed in spring.

▣ ◊ ✾✾✾

Recommended: *G. paniculata* 'Bristol Fairy' ♀.

RECOMMENDED GRASSES

Briza (Quaking grass)
Medium-sized, with dainty spikelets rising out of blue-green tufts of leaves in summer. Divide in spring.
⬛ ◊ ✳✳✳ *B. media p.35.*

Carex (Sedge)
Tufts of green, gold, bronze or striped leaves; catkin-like flowers in summer. Heights vary. Divide in spring.
⬛ ⬛ ◊ or ◊ ✳✳✳ *C. pendula p.35.*

Cortaderia (Pampas grass)
Tall, architectural, with silver plumes in late summer. Cover crowns with straw in winter.
⬛ ◊ ✳✳

Hakonechloa
Small, low mounds of green and gold leaves; red autumn tints. Good in containers.
⬛ ◊ ✳✳✳

Miscanthus
Tall, elegant, invaluable in mixed plantings or as a specimen. Some have striped leaves. Silky, late summer flowerheads can be left to decorate the winter garden. Divide in spring.
⬛ ◊ ✳✳✳
Recommended: *M. sinensis* ♀.

Stipa
Medium-to-tall grasses, often with a lax but attractive

HAKONECHLOA MACRA '*AUREOLA*'

habit. Sprays of oat-like or feathery flowers appear from mid-summer. These are good for drying. Divide in spring.
⬛ ◊ ✳✳✳
Recommended: *S. gigantea.*

H

Helenium
Medium-sized, clump-forming plants with yellow, orange, red and bronze daisy-like flowers from summer to early autumn. Good for cutting. Divide in autumn or spring.
⬛ ◊ ✳✳✳
H. 'Coppelia' p.30.

Helianthus (Sunflower)
Several tall perennials as well as the familiar, annual type. Perennials have smaller double or single yellow flowers. Divide in spring or autumn.
⬛ ◊ ✳✳✳
H. 'Loddon Gold' ♀ p.29.

Helleborus (Hellebore)
Small plants, highly valued for their winter and spring flowers in white, cream, pink,

purple or green, some spotted maroon. Handsome foliage. Cut back old leaves as flowers open. Sow seed as it ripens.
⬛ ◊ ✳✳✳
H. orientalis p.38;
H. × ericsmithii p.12.

Hemerocallis (Daylily)
Showy flowers in yellow, pink, orange or red, borne in medium-height clumps all summer. Flowers last only a day but appear in rapid succession. Strap-like foliage

HELLEBORUS ORIENTALIS

is sometimes evergreen. Many hybrids. Divide in spring.
⬛ ◊ ✳✳✳

Heuchera (Coral flower)
Semi-evergreen or evergreen, low, ground-cover plants, with leaves coloured green, bronze or purple. Narrow spires of tiny white, pink or red flowers appear in summer. Divide in autumn.
⬛ ◊ ✳✳✳
H. micrantha 'Palace Purple' ♀ p.46.

Hosta (Plantain lily)
Low but dense clumps of large, heart-shaped leaves, often blue-green or marked with cream or gold, ideal as ground cover. Spikes of tubular flowers are a bonus in summer. Divide in early spring.
⬛ ◊ ✳✳✳
H. 'Shade Fanfare' ♀ pp.40, 43; H. sieboldiana p.38.

I

IRIS 'BROWN LASSO'

Iris
Very many small- to medium-sized plants with differing requirements. Bearded irises (*as above*) need sun and free-draining soil. They come in a wide range of colours with plenty of bicolours; some have ruffled petals. Other irises, such as Siberian irises (*I. sibirica)* and *I. laevigata*, need moist soil and are useful for borders and waterside schemes. Divide Siberian irises in spring; bearded irises in mid- to late summer after flowering.
◻ ◊◊ ✱✱✱
I. sibirica p.43.

K

Knautia macedonica
Medium-sized plants with scabious-like, deep crimson, pincushion flowers in summer. Good in informal plantings. Take basal cuttings or sow seed in spring.
◻ ◊ ✱✱✱

Kniphofia (Red-hot poker)
Dazzling, medium to tall spikes of tubular red, orange or yellow flowers are held well above clumps of strap-shaped leaves in summer. Mulch with straw in first winter. Divide in spring.
◻ ◊ ✱✱✱
K. rooperi p.2.

L

Lamium (Deadnettle)
This useful, small, ground-cover plant bears white, pink or purple flowers in late spring. Some have gold- or silver-splashed leaves. Divide in spring or take cuttings in early summer.
▨ ◊ ✱✱✱

Leucanthemum
White or yellow daisy-like flowers, sometimes quite shaggy-looking, are produced in summer on clump- or mat-forming plants. Divide or sow seed in spring or autumn.
◻ ◊ ✱✱✱
L. vulgare p.35.

Liatris
Summer- to autumn-flowering plants, with medium-to-tall spikes of small, tufted, white or purple flowers. Divide in spring, or sow seed in autumn.
◻ ◊ ✱✱✱

Ligularia
Large, robust, with tall heads of yellow or orange flowers in mid- to late summer. Excellent by water. Some have leaves with purple undersides. Divide in spring or autumn.
◻▨ ◊ ✱✱✱
Recommended: *L. dentata* 'Desdemona' ✿

Linum (Flax)
Small- to medium-sized plants with yellow or blue flowers in spring and summer. Sow seed in autumn or take stem-tip cuttings in summer.
◻ ◊ ✱✱✱
Recommended: *L. narbonense.*

Lobelia
Perennials are quite different from bedding lobelia: medium-height border plants, they appreciate damp ground. Spires of red, pink or rich purple flowers are borne from late summer to mid-autumn. Foliage can be purplish-red. Divide in spring. Borderline hardy; dry-mulch to protect crowns in winter.
◻ ◊ ✱✱
Recommended: *L. cardinalis* ✿, *L.* 'Queen Victoria' ✿

Lunaria rediviva (Honesty)
The biennial honesty is most commonly grown, but this perennial is an attractive plant of medium height with white or lilac fragrant flowers from late spring. Silvery seed pods dry well. Divide in spring or sow seed in autumn or spring.
▨ ◊ ✱✱✱

LIATRIS SPICATA 'KOBOLD'

LUPINUS 'CHANDELIER'

Lupinus (Lupin)
Elegant, medium-height spikes of pea-like flowers in a wide range of colours appear in summer above attractively divided leaves. Many are bicoloured. Will self-seed but seedlings may not be like their parent. Take basal cuttings in mid-spring.
◻ ◊ ✱✱✱

Lychnis
Tall, upright, clump-forming plants bear white, pink, red or purple star-shaped flowers, singly or in clusters, in summer. Divide and take basal cuttings in spring, sow seed as soon as it ripens.
◻ ◊ ✱✱✱
L. chalcedonica ♀ *p.28.*
Also recommended:
L. coronaria Alba Group ♀

Lysimachia (Loosestrife)
Most types bear tall, upright spires of small, star-shaped flowers in summer in white or yellow. Good for informal plantings. Sow seed in spring, divide in spring or autumn.
◻ ◊ ✱✱✱
Recommended:
L. clethroides ♀, *L. punctata.*

M

Macleaya (Plume poppy)
Tall plants producing a profuse summer display of tiny, tubular, cream and coral-pink flowers, in airy plumes above greyish, heart-shaped leaves. Sow seed in spring, or divide in spring or autumn.
◻ ◊ ✱✱✱
M. microcarpa 'Kelway's Coral Plume' ♀ *pp.32, 35.*

Malva (Mallow)
Easily grown plants of medium height bearing saucer-shaped flowers in white, pink or blue from late spring to mid-autumn. Take basal cuttings in spring, or sow seed in spring or summer.
◻ ◊ ✱✱✱
Recommended: *M. moschata* f. *alba* ♀

Meconopsis
Poppy-like flowers, especially suitable for wildflower gardens or woodland settings. The tall, blue Himalayan types – *M. betonicifolia*, *M. grandis* – are less easy to grow than the small yellow or orange Welsh poppy, *M. cambrica*. Most prefer slightly acid soil. Plants can be short-lived. Divide after flowering.
✳ ◻ ◊ ✱✱✱

Mimulus (Monkey flower)
There are several small hardy perennial mimulus bearing colourful snapdragon-like flowers from spring to summer. These may be white, yellow, red or pink. Often short-lived. Divide in spring.
◻ ◊◊ ✱✱ ✱✱✱
M. cupreus 'Whitecroft Scarlet' ♀ *p.42.*

MONARDA 'BEAUTY OF COBHAM'

Monarda (Bergamot)
Clump-forming, medium-sized plants with densely packed heads of colourful tubular flowers from mid-summer to early autumn. Mainly shades of red, pink and purple. Aromatic foliage; the flowers attract bees. Take basal cuttings or divide in spring, or sow seed in spring or autumn.
◻ ◊ ✱✱✱
Recommended: *M.* 'Beauty of Cobham' ♀, *M.* 'Cambridge Scarlet' ♀

N

Nepeta (Catmint)
Small- to medium-sized plants bearing clusters of usually blue flowers in summer and early autumn. Good for softening border edges. Aromatic leaves are grey-green. Attractive to bees and often to cats. Cut back after first flowering to encourage a second flush. Divide in spring or autumn, take stem-tip or basal cuttings in early summer.
◻ ◊ ✱✱✱
Recommended: *N.* × *faassenii*, *N. sibirica.*

O

Oenothera
(Evening primrose)
Upright or trailing small-to-medium plants bear profuse but short-lived summer displays of fragrant yellow, white or pink flowers. Divide or sow seed in spring, take stem tip cuttings in late spring.
▣ ◊ ✳✳✳
Recommended: *O. fruticosa* 'Fyrverkeri' ♀

Omphalodes
Small, semi-evergreen or evergreen ground-cover plants, bearing small blue flowers in spring and early summer. Divide or sow seed in spring.
▧▨ ◊ ✳✳✳
O. verna p.38.
Also recommended:
O. cappadocica ♀

P

Paeonia (Peony)
Medium-sized clumps of handsome foliage with sumptuous double or single

PAEONIA OFFICINALIS
'CRIMSON GLOBE'

flowers in white, pink, red and rarely yellow, from late spring to mid-summer. May need support. Long-lived but resent disturbance. Divide in autumn or early spring, or take root cuttings in winter.
▣ ◊ ✳✳✳

Papaver (Poppy)
Perennials, flowering from early summer, range from the flamboyant, medium-height red, pink or white oriental types to the small yellow and orange alpine poppies. Divide or sow seed in spring, take root cuttings in winter.
▣ ◊ ✳✳✳
P. orientale p.48.

Penstemon
Medium-sized, clump-forming plants, with spires of foxglove-like flowers in white and shades of pink, red and purple from mid-summer to autumn. Take cuttings in summer. Borderline hardy.
▣ ◊ ✳✳

Persicaria
Small-to-medium ground-cover plants, which can be invasive, with spikes of tiny white, pink and red flowers in summer. Sow seed or take stem tip cuttings in spring, divide in spring or autumn.
▣ ◊ ✳✳✳
P. bistorta 'Superba' *pp.40, 42.*

Phlomis
Small range of medium-sized perennials bearing tubular yellow or pink summer flowers in dense, circular clusters around upright stems. The seedheads are decorative in winter. Divide in spring.
▣ ◊ ✳✳✳
Recommended: *P. russeliana* ♀

PHLOX PANICULATA
'GRAF ZEPPELIN'

Phlox
Many medium-to-tall border phlox to choose from, bearing clusters of white, pink, red, lilac or purple, lightly fragrant flowers, generally towards late summer. Numerous small phlox are grown as rock plants. Take root cuttings in autumn.
▣ ◊ ✳✳✳

Phormium
Tall, architectural evergreen plants grown for their sword-like green, bronze or striped leaves. Can be used to make focal points in a garden. Divide in spring. Borderline hardiness; can be protected in winter by wrapping in hessian or bubble-wrap.
▣ ◊ ✳✳
Recommended:
P. cookianum ♀, *P. tenax* ♀

Physostegia
Upright plant of medium height, bearing spikes of tubular white, pink or purple flowers in summer. Good for cutting. Divide in winter or early spring.
▣ ◊ ✳✳✳

Polemonium (Jacob's ladder)
Small, clump-forming plants, with clusters of usually blue, sometimes pink or white, flowers in spring and summer. Divide in spring, sow seed in spring or autumn.
▣ ◊ ✳✳✳
Recommended: *P.* 'Lambrook Mauve' ♀

Polygonatum
(Solomon's seal)
Medium-to-tall arching stems of white or cream bells in summer suit shady borders or woodland. Divide in spring.
✱ ◊◊ ✳✳✳
P. falcatum 'Variegatum' *p.38*

Primula
Vast range includes moisture-loving candelabra primulas, such as *P. japonica*, as well as those with familiar primrose-like flowers. Small, clump-forming plants, they are perfect in informal settings and lightly shaded borders. Numerous colours, some with double flowers. Divide in early autumn, or sow seed as soon as it ripens.
▣ ◊ ✳✳✳
P. japonica ♀ *p.42.*

PRIMULA 'MISS INDIGO'

Pulmonaria (Lungwort)
Small, spreading clumps of silver-spotted leaves, with blue, pink or white flowers in spring. Leaf markings vary. Divide in autumn; take root cuttings in winter.
✱ ◊ ✳✳✳

Pulsatilla (Pasque flower)
Small, with ferny leaves and silky purple or white flowers in spring. Silky seedheads follow. Must have a sunny, sheltered, free-draining site. Sow seed when ripe.
▣ ◊ ✳✳✳
P. vulgaris ♀ *p.47.*

R

Ranunculus
Apart from rock plants, the best-known perennial species is the small *R. aconitifolius*, with dainty white flowers on branching stems. Divide in spring or autumn.
▣ ◊ ✳✳✳
Recommended: *R. aconitifolius* 'Flore Pleno' ♀

Rheum
Tall, imposing plants with large, coarsely toothed and veined leaves. Tall plumes of tiny, usually red or cream flowers in early summer. Divide in spring.
▣ ◊ ✳✳✳
Recommended: *R. palmatum* ♀

Rudbeckia (Coneflower)
Medium-to-tall plants with colourful, mainly yellow, daisy-like flowers in summer and autumn. Good for cutting. Sow seed in spring, divide in spring or autumn.
▣ ◊◊ ✳✳✳
R. laciniata p.34.

S

Salvia
Several hardy perennials, suiting a variety of sites, but usually needing sun and good drainage. Medium-height summer spikes of flowers are generally purple, pink, blue or white; leaves are aromatic. Divide in spring.
▣ ◊ ✳✳✳
S. × superba ♀ *p.31.*

Scabiosa (Scabious)
Attractive blue, pink, lemon or white flowers with pincushion centres are borne in summer on wiry stems. Small-to-medium plants. Divide in spring or autumn.
▣ ◊ ✳✳✳
Recommended: *S. caucasica* 'Clive Greaves' ♀

Schizostylis coccinea
(Kaffir lily)
Upright spikes of white, pink or red flowers, good for cutting, appear late summer to early winter. Medium-sized plants with strap-shaped leaves. Divide in spring.
▣ ◊ ✳✳✳

SCABIOSA 'BUTTERFLY BLUE'

Sedum

Fleshy-leaved plants with clusters of small, star-shaped, usually red or pink flowers in summer and autumn. Foliage sometimes tinted purple or grey. Small- to medium-sized plants, the latter ones having a rather lax habit. Sedums also include several rock plants. Divide in spring.

✿ ◊ ✽✽✽
S. 'Ruby Glow' ♀ *p.31*;
S. *spectabile* 'Brilliant' ♀ *p.17*.

Sidalcea (False mallow)

Medium-sized, clump-forming plants with spires of hollyhock-like pink or white flowers produced from early to late summer. These last well when cut. Divide in early spring; take basal stem cuttings in spring.

✿ ◊ ✽✽✽

Sisyrinchium striatum

Fan-shaped clumps of lance-shaped evergreen leaves, striped cream in 'Aunt May', bear sturdy spikes of cream flowers in summer. Small- to medium-sized plants; there are also several small sisyrinchiums for rock

SIDALCEA 'OBERON'

SISYRINCHIUM STRIATUM 'AUNT MAY'

gardens. Divide in spring or sow seed in autumn.

✿ ◊ ✽✽✽

Solidago (Goldenrod)

Medium-to-tall plants bearing plumes of tiny gold flowers from mid-summer to autumn. The species are rather coarse and invasive and best in a wild garden, but the named hybrids are suited to borders. Divide in autumn or spring.

✿ ◊ ✽✽✽
Recommended:
S. 'Goldenmosa' ♀

Stachys

Low, spreading plants, good for ground cover or a border's edge. Lambs' ears (S. *byzantina*) is grown for its evergreen, silver, woolly leaves and S. *macrantha* for its dense spikes of purple-pink flowers in summer. Divide or sow seed in spring.

✿ ◊ ✽✽✽

Symphytum (Comfrey)

Small-to-medium, vigorous plants that make good ground cover in wild and woodland gardens. Coarse, hairy leaves

SYMPHYTUM 'GOLDSMITH'

are at their best variegated (*as above*). Flowers, in late spring and summer, come in shades of blue, cream, pink or purple. Divide in spring.

✿ ◊ ✽✽✽
Also recommended: S. × *uplandicum* 'Variegatum' ♀

T

Tanacetum

Pink or red daisy flowers of pyrethrum (T. *coccineum*) are useful in a border in early summer, and make good cut flowers. White-flowered feverfew (T. *parthenium*) is suited to border edges or informal plantings. There are also several small, silver-leaved rock species. Sow seed or divide in spring.

✿ ◊ ✽✽✽

Thalictrum (Meadow rue)

Attractive plants with delicate foliage, often blue-green, and sprays of tiny, tufted flowers. Those medium to tall in height are ideal for borders or more informal plantings. Flower colours include white, pink, mauve and lemon. Some

TIARELLA TRIFOLIATA

prefer cool, damp sites. Sow seed or divide in spring.
🔲 ◊ ◊ ✳✳✳
Recommended: *T. delavayi* 'Hewitt's Double' ♀, *T. flavum* subsp. *glaucum* ♀

Tiarella (Foam flower)
Superb ground-cover plants for light shade; leaves colour well in autumn. Airy clusters of tiny, star-shaped, pink or white flowers are borne from spring to summer. Sow seed or divide in spring or autumn.
🔲 ◊ ✳✳✳
T. wherryi ♀ *p.39.* Also recommended: *T. trifoliata.*

Tradescantia
Small plants with dense clumps of fleshy stems and strap-shaped leaves. Although the 3-petalled flowers, in white, pink, purple or blue, are short-lived, they are produced in long succession. Divide in spring or autumn.
🔲 ◊ ✳✳✳
Recommended: *T. × andersonia* 'Isis' ♀

Tricyrtis (Toad lily)
Curious-looking funnel- or star-shaped flowers in white,

yellow or pinkish-purple, often spotted, appear in late summer and autumn on medium-sized, shade-loving plants. Divide in spring.
🔲 ▣ ◊ ✳✳✳
Recommended:
T. formosana ♀

Trollius (Globeflower)
Medium-sized plants bear buttercup-like lemon or yellow flowers in spring or summer above clumps of deeply divided leaves. Needs moist soil; good in pondside plantings. Divide after flowering.
🔲 ◊ ✳✳✳
T. europaeus p.43.

V

Verbascum (Mullein)
Spikes of flowers, yellow or sometimes white, purple or pink, rise from rosettes of leaves, often grey and woolly. Height varies greatly. Sow seed or divide in spring, take root cuttings in winter.
🔲 ◊ ✳✳✳
V. chaixii 'Gainsborough' ♀ *p.30.*

VERBASCUM 'COTSWOLD QUEEN'

Verbena bonariensis
Tall, wiry stems bear flattened heads of tiny, purple flowers in summer and autumn. Very effective in mixed, informal plantings. Borderline hardy, but often flowers in first season if sown in early spring.
🔲 ◊ ✳✳

Veronica
Generally small, low-growing plants bearing upright spikes of small flowers, usually in shades of blue, sometimes pink, from late spring to summer. Divide in spring or autumn, sow seed in autumn.
🔲 ◊ ✳✳✳
Recommended:
V. gentianoides ♀

Viola
Delightful small plants with flowers, sometimes scented, in a wide range of colours. Deadhead to encourage more flowers; cut back in autumn to keep in shape, especially *V. cornuta.* Sow seed in spring; take stem tip cuttings in spring or late summer.
🔲 ▣ ◊ ✳✳✳
V. riviniana Purpurea Group *p.46.*

VERONICA LONGIFOLIA

INDEX

ACKNOWLEDGMENTS

Picture research Sean Hunter

Special photography Peter Anderson

Illustrations Gill Tomblin

Additional illustrations Karen Cochrane

Index Hilary Bird

Dorling Kindersley would like to thank:
All staff at the RHS, in particular Susanne Mitchell, Karen Wilson and Barbara Haynes at Vincent Square; Candida Frith-Macdonald for editorial assistance.

The Royal Horticultural Society
To learn more about the work of the Society, visit the RHS on the Internet at **www.rhs.org.uk**. Information includes news of events around the country, a horticultural database, international plant registers, results of plant trials and membership details.

Photography
The publisher would like to thank the following for their kind permission to reproduce their photographs:
(key: a=above; b=below; c=centre; l=left; r=right; t=top)

Garden Picture Library: Brigitte Thomas 18b; Howard Rice 12br, 23tl; J. S. Sira front cover crb, 16b, 16cra, 43tc; Steven Wooster 25tl; Sunniva Harte 12bl
John Glover: 2, 8b, 9tl, 14br, 22b, 44
Jerry Harpur: 6, 7br, 9br, 11br, 14clb, 48
Andrew Lawson: front cover cr, cla, back cover c, tr, tl, 9cra, 10b, 15tr, 23r, 32, 33br, 36, 37br
Clive Nichols: front cover r, 13tl, 15tl; Little Bowden, Berkshire 26; Tintinhull Gardens, Somerset 11tl
Planet Earth Pictures: Steve Hopkin 62br
Howard Rice: 19t, 19bl
Harry Smith Collection: 37bl